ON PLAYING A
POOR HAND WELL

Insights
from the
Lives
of Those
Who Have
Overcome
Childhood
Risks and
Adversities

Mark Katz, Ph.D.

W. W. Norton & Company
New York • London

Composition by Bytheway Typesetting Services, Inc.
Manufacturing by Haddon Craftsmen, Inc.

Library of Congress Cataloging-in-Publication Data

Katz, Mark, 1949–
    On playing a poor hand well : insights from the lives of those who
have overcome childhood risks and adversities / Mark Katz.
        p.   cm.
    Includes bibliographical references and index.
    ISBN 0-393-70232-4
    1. Stress in children.   2. Resilience (Personality trait) in
children.   3. Psychic trauma in children.   4. Adjustment
(Psychology)   5. Child welfare.   I. Title.
RJ507.S77K38   1997
155.9′083−dc20   96-38185   CIP

W. W. Norton & Company, Inc., 500 Fifth Avenue, New York, N.Y. 10110
http://www.wwnorton.com
W. W. Norton & Company, Ltd., 10 Coptic Street, London WC1A 1PU

1   2   3   4   5   6   7   8   9   0

To Terri

Contents

PART II
BEATING THE ODDS

PART III
CHANGING THE ODDS

Acknowledgments

The time is late December, a few days before Christmas, and the following individuals have just unwrapped a colorfully decorated package. In the package they have found a copy of this book. And as they flip the pages to the acknowledgments section they are seeing their names in print here for the first time. They are reading about how much I cherish their friendship and support, about how instrumental they were in helping me complete this book, and about how much Terri and I are thinking of them this holiday season. Merry Christmas to Ken Heying, Roland Rotz, Amy Ellis, Clare Jones, Mary Lou Evans, Jeff Rowe, Martha Hillyard, Dorothy Johnson, and Michael Rybak for the encouragement you've provided to me over the years, and for the extraordinary work you do to help others. You are truly gifted people.

I would also like to extend my thanks to Susan Barrows Munro, Director of Norton Professional Books, and Regina Dahlgren Ardini, Associate Editor, for your support and guidance throughout the writing of this book.

And finally to Paul and Barbara Hunter. There are no words that I can think of to adequately convey the debt of gratitude that I and others owe to you for your unwavering commitment to an improved system of care.

Introduction

Robert Louis Stevenson once said, "Life is not so much a matter of holding good cards, but sometimes of playing a poor hand well." Many adults who currently enjoy happy and productive lives grew up under very difficult and emotionally stressful conditions that they couldn't change, no matter how hard they tried. Some of these individuals managed to escape serious emotional damage entirely, to defy the odds, so to speak. Others struggled as children and teenagers with serious emotional, behavioral, and school difficulties, and then turned their lives around in their twenties.

What did these individuals need to endure? Where did they find the strength and resilience? Were they shielded and protected in special ways? If so, by whom? What turned things around for them? What do they see as their turning point experiences or second-chance opportunities?

Researchers studying the life trajectories of individuals exposed to childhood risk factors are learning a great deal about how some individuals "beat the odds" and about how some others, after years of suffering, manage to turn their lives around. While there is still much to learn about the positive life trajectories of individuals such as these, much has already been learned. And this knowledge may prove very helpful to children, families, and young adults now confronting many of the same risks and adversities.

This book begins the process of integrating this knowledge into practice. I almost wrote *clinical* practice, but then realized that so much of what is reviewed here involves attending to protective influences that aren't usually considered part of routine clinical practice. Hopefully, this will change. Research has shown that the protective influences we're going to discuss, while not routinely addressed by educators, mental health professionals, and other service providers, have nonetheless been instrumental in helping some of our most at risk children, families, and young adults overcome multiple adversities. John McNight (1989) once said that educational and psychological interventions aren't the only ways to respond to the human condition. As we learn more about how vulnerable children grow into successful adults, and the role certain protective processes play in this regard, those words will begin to take on a special new meaning.

New Insights into Childhood Risks and Adversities

The book begins with a discussion of new insights into a range of childhood risks and adversities that are now recognized as beyond a child's ability to alter, no matter how hard he or she tries. They're inescapable and enduring. Trying harder won't make them go away. The child's job is to adapt as best as he or she can. Witnessing up close the sights and sounds of violent relationships at home, being abused physically, sexually, or emotionally by a family member, growing up in a very violent and dangerous neighborhood, going from foster home to foster home or placement to placement—they're all on the list of risks and adversities that reflect "Exposure to Inescapable, Enduring, and Potentially Traumatizing Experiences," the title of chapter 1.

Add to this list children who experience attention difficulties and learning disabilities. From the first day of first grade, the vulnerabilities that these children experience may prevent them from learning and behaving like most other children, even though they desperately want nothing more than to be like everyone else. They may look like they can do the work. Many may have intellectual gifts of one form or another. Yet, despite their best efforts, they don't learn like most other children. Our customary response? Try harder, you'll do better. No, they won't. For these children, the first day of first grade can be the start of an enduring, humiliating experience from which there is no escape. New insights into the nature of attention difficulties and learning disabilities, as well as our increased awareness of what children experiencing these conditions often go through emotionally is the focus of chapter 2.

Some risks and adversities are environmental in nature. Others are neurobiological. Environmental risks are events, experiences, or conditions that surround the child and his or her family. Living in impoverished surroundings, witnessing a great deal of violence, being abused physically, sexually, or emotionally, having no one around who can care for the child or keep him or her safe are all examples of environmental risks and adversities. The conditions explored in chapter 1 relate to these types of risks. Neurobiological risks, on the other hand, refer to conditions believed to be physical or neurochemical in nature. Researchers now speak of a variety of childhood disorders that stem from neurobiological causes, disorders that many people used to think were due solely to environmental factors. The list of childhood disorders with identifiable physical and neurobiological causes keeps growing. Chapter 2 focuses on two neurobiological risks — perhaps the two most common sources of vulnerability in childhood: attention-deficit/ hyperactivity disorder and learning disabilities.

Try as the child may to endure exposure to inescapable, stressful conditions, be they environmental, neurobiological, or a combination of both, he or she often pays a heavy price, psychologically and physiologically. And herein lies the awful paradox. Rarely will this child be able to communicate his pain in a language we can understand. He may blame himself and communicate his feelings through his behavior. If and when this behavior becomes disruptive, he is likely to be punished or reprimanded. We may come to see this child's emotional and behavioral displays as the result of deeply rooted psychological difficulties. He may be labeled as severely emotionally disturbed and treated as such.

Are these children severely emotionally disturbed? What's normal behavior under these circumstances? Are we aware of the potential emotional and behavioral effects that exposure to inescapable, enduring, and overwhelmingly stressful conditions can have upon a child? And have we ever examined the consequences of treating the resulting emotional and behavioral displays that arise from a child's attempts to adapt to these conditions as being due to oppositional motives? Or as emerging character flaws?

These questions are asked in Part I. In the remaining parts, I will discuss why the manner in which we answer these questions can literally determine whether vulnerable children and families are provided with, or deprived of, the sources of strength and protection that allow many individuals to endure and overcome similar risks and adversities.

Beating the Odds

We know all too well that risks and adversities have a way of piling up. They can occur together. As a result, many children and families have to confront multiple risks and adversities. Overcoming multiple adversities can be much more difficult than overcoming one source of stress or exposure to one specific risk. Chapters 3 and 4 discuss what researchers have learned about children who, despite being exposed to multiple risks, were able to overcome these conditions, and go on to enjoy productive lives as adults. How did they do it? What were some turning points? The answers to these questions help open our minds to a very important reality: Significant and positive changes occur throughout the lifespan in response to many different experiences.

Changing the Odds

Emmy Werner and Michael Rutter, two of the leading researchers in the field of human resilience, provide a framework for changing the odds of those who have been dealt a poor hand. They have synthesized some of the research findings in the field of human resilience with some of their own findings and have defined a series of four broad-based protective influences that have been instrumental in helping individuals overcome a range of childhood adversities. Part III reviews these protective influences and presents ways to incorporate them into the lives of vulnerable children, families, and young adults.

Chapters 5 and 6 highlight the first of the four protective processes, which involves experiences and conditions that reduce the impact of the prevailing risks on children and families. There are two ways to minimize this impact: learning to see one's adversities in a new light and providing buffers, or protective shields, during critical parts of each day (Rutter, 1990). Finding the right words, the right language, to legitimize and validate the pain in one's life allows for hardships and adversities to be viewed in a new light. For those who have endured exposure to traumatic life circumstances it also allows the recovery process to begin and helps restore a sense of psychological integrity (Pynoos, 1991).

Researchers are identifying ways in which community resources and social supports are serving as protective shields for children and families throughout the day. Some researchers also feel that there may be no greater resource than the neighborhood school for protecting, nourishing, and stimulating children raised under conditions of severe adversity (Garmezy, 1991; Rutter, 1979a).

Sometimes, you just can't stop things from spiraling out of control. Those having to endure exposure to multiple hardships are at greater risk of having things spiral out of control than others. Children and families caught in this downward spiral need some type of "safety net" to break their fall and allow them to regain a sense of control and stability in their lives. These safety nets comprise the second protective process and are detailed in chapter 7.

Chapter 8 focuses on the third protective process, which involves experiences that serve to develop a sense of mastery and self-efficacy. Successful individuals who overcame earlier adversities were often able to define themselves more around their multiple talents than around their areas of vulnerability. Being able to showcase our talents and to have them valued by those who are important to us helps us define our identities around that which we do best. This chapter will discuss ways in which some schools are helping children recognize and express their diverse talents, so that their identities can be formed around their strengths.

Chapter 9 is devoted to the last of the broad protective processes: turning points, or specific experiences in people's lives that offer important opportunities for change. There are many different examples of turning points. For some children, starting school can be a turning point. For teenagers and young adults, obtaining a specific job that highlights their strengths or talents could represent a turning point. Some young adults have identified joining the armed services as a turning point. Others cite an important new relationship that turned their lives around. Michael Rutter (1990) believes that some people have greater access to potential turning point experiences and therefore may be offered greater protection than others. By being aware of the important role that turning point experiences and second-chance opportunities have had in the lives of those who overcame childhood adversities, we're much more likely to provide avenues through which they may occur.

We are learning a great deal from those who have fought hard to overcome the adversities and hardships they faced as children, those who have beat the odds. However, for some, the odds will be insurmountable; all the strength, courage, and resilience that they muster won't be enough to overcome them. The odds will be too great. They'll have to change. And, thanks to our new insights into childhood risks and adversities and into the lives of those who overcame them, we're now capable of changing the odds for many vulnerable children, families, and young adults in ways that we were never able to before. Incorporating this new research and knowledge into our system of care and, more importantly, into our hearts and minds remains our greatest challenge.

ON PLAYING A
POOR HAND WELL

Life is not always a matter of holding good cards,
but sometimes of playing a poor hand well.

Robert Louis Stevenson

Part I

New Insights into Childhood Risks and Adversities

During the period of slavery in America, a Louisiana doctor by the name of Samuel W. Cartwright believed that some slaves suffered from a specific kind of mental disorder, or "disease of the mind," which he referred to as *drapetomania* (Stampp, 1956). One of the symptoms of drapetomania was a sulky and dissatisfied attitude. The disease also caused some slaves to run away. Slaves who visibly showed their displeasure over living in bondage, and those who chose to risk death by running away rather than continue to live as slaves, were seen as suffering from a disease of the mind. They were seen by Dr. Cartwright as mentally ill.

Chapter 1

Exposure to Inescapable, Enduring, and Potentially Traumatizing Experiences

In 1993, a colleague who was extremely knowledgeable about the effects of domestic violence on children gave an inservice presentation to a small group of educators and mental health professionals at a mental health treatment center in San Diego, California. The presenter's hope was that professionals who work with children and families would realize the potentially traumatizing effects that exposure to domestic violence can have on children. As part of her inservice, the presenter played an audiotape recording of a 911 call that a child made. The child was crying uncontrollably, begging the 911 operator for help, saying that his father is beating up his mother and he's afraid that his father is going to kill her. His mother was crying hysterically in the background. The child tells the operator that this goes on all the time, whenever his father comes home drunk. He is screaming into the phone, "Somebody help me."

I was part of that group attending this inservice presentation. As we listened to the tape recording, we felt ourselves growing numb. When the tape ended no one spoke. If it had not ended at that time, someone would have asked to shut it off. The child's plea for help and his uncontrollable crying were too difficult to listen to. We all were privately thinking the same thing: Somebody do something to help this poor child.

The presenter made her point in a very powerful way. Hearing what exposure to domestic violence sounds like is different from reading about it in a report, when a distance can be established. Hearing it live, while it's happening, triggers an entirely different level of emotion.

We know that exposure to domestic violence represents only one of many different ways that children can be traumatized by overwhelming and inescapable events. Researchers are also uncovering the potentially traumatizing effects of sexual abuse, physical abuse, and emotional neglect (Famularo, Kinscherff, & Fenton, 1992; Kiser, Heston, Millsap, & Pruitt, 1991; McLeer, Deblinger, Henry, & Orvaschel, 1992; Wolfe, Gentile, & Wolfe, 1989); of growing up in violent and dangerous neighborhoods (Garbarino, 1991); and of multiple out-of-home placements that some children must endure when they are no longer able to live at home (Doyle & Bauer, 1989). Children exposed to ongoing, inescapable traumatic experiences have to adapt as best they can to conditions that they can't control.

Their best efforts, however, are often not enough to prevent serious psychological and physiological consequences. Some children develop wide-ranging symptoms consistent with what researchers have come to associate with posttraumatic stress disorder. Other children may develop some of the symptoms of posttraumatic stress disorder, but not the full spectrum (McLeer et al., 1992). Still others may develop an entirely different set of symptoms (Lyons, 1987).

Over time, children may begin to feel that there's no future for them. James Garbarino (1994) refers to this as terminal thinking. He observed this phenomenon in children around the world who were growing up in war zones and a very similar phenomenon in children growing up in violent urban areas of the United States.

Exposure to extremely stressful conditions that one can't change or escape from can have profound effects on anyone, regardless of age. It can alter how we see the world, how we see others, and how we perceive our own worth. The effects may be especially severe in children because children lack perspective (Terr, 1990). They have nothing to compare their circumstances to. It can appear as though there really is no alternative; this is how it's going to be. The child tries over and over again to alter the painful and frustrating circumstances he finds himself in, but to no avail. It's beyond his ability to control. His job now is to try and adapt as best he can.

Escapable versus Inescapable Stress

The inescapability of stress, be it real or perceived, exerts a particularly high price on our psychological and physiological integrity. Studies in the area of learned helplessness have shown that if an individual tries to alter a situation over and over again to no avail, it's not unusual for him to just stop trying. He learns that he is helpless to change things. Hopelessness and depression may follow (Peterson, Maier, & Seligman, 1993). Physiological research studies on animals exposed to harmless levels of shock showed that exposure to uncontrollable and inescapable shock had very different effects on an animal's central nervous system than shock that the animal could control and escape from. Inescapable shock had significantly more severe effects. In fact, being able to control the shock produced a kind of stress resistance (van der Kolk & Greenberg, 1987).

The Effects of Overwhelming and Inescapable Stress

Bruce Perry, one of the researchers studying the psychological and physiological consequences of exposure to overwhelming stress, explains that after a person is exposed to a traumatic experience, he wants to return to normal, but his brain may be replaying the event over and over, trying to make some sense of what happened (McCormick, 1993). Physiologically, he can go into a state of "permanent overdrive" and become overly vigilant, looking for signs of danger. He may also try to short-circuit the alarm signals his brain is giving off by going numb—but while his face may look emotionless or bleak, states Perry, his heart is pounding and his brain is screaming "Danger!" (cited by McCormick).

The Awful Paradox

In trying to make sense of the enormity of a traumatizing experience, adults are likely to use logic. Children are less logical; they're more likely to blame themselves for what's happening to them. Many will also act out their pain behaviorally and emotionally. And herein lies the awful paradox. Children exposed to inescapable and overwhelming stress that they can't control, no matter how hard they try, often don't talk to us about it. They don't scream their pain out in a language we can understand, like that little boy making the 911 call did. If these children were capable of doing this, we would respond to them in entirely different ways. We would buffer them, give them the perspective they lack, and change their circumstances immediately. Instead, children often suffer silently. If they act out their pain with disruptive behavior, we may come to see it as willful or oppositional and be inclined to punish them. This should come as no surprise. Research has shown that if we think an individual (child or adult) has complete control over his actions, over how things turn out, it can potentially evoke anger in us (Weiner, 1993). It increases the likelihood of punishment or rejection on our part. We're much less likely to offer help. On the other hand, if we think that the individual (child or adult) does not have complete control over certain actions or outcomes, we're much more likely to respond sympathetically, to reach out and help in some way (Weiner).

Not realizing that children exposed to inescapable, overwhelming stress may act out their pain, that they may misbehave, not listen to us, or seek our attention in all the wrong ways, can lead us to punish these children for their misbehavior. The behavior is so willful, so intentional. She controlled herself yesterday, she can control herself today. If we only knew what happened last night, or this morning before she got to school, we would be shielding the same child we're now reprimanding.

Lessons Learned from Veterans of Vietnam

On July 4, 1994, a parade marched through a beautiful park in an affluent area of southern California. Marching in the parade were some proud veterans of WWII who were cheered on by an appreciative crowd of spectators, who, over a half century later, still honored them for their heroism. The veterans marched by a middle-aged man, unshaven, dirty, curled up under a nearby tree. He was barely awake. Actually, he lives under that tree, surviving on pennies, dimes, and quarters from people who pass by. He's also a veteran—of Vietnam. He served as much time in his war as the WWII veterans served in theirs. He witnessed similar horrors, felt just as much terror, came just as close to death, lived through just as much enduring, inescapable, and often overwhelming stress. The only real difference was the experience of coming home. The WWII veterans were showered with love and affection; they came back heroes. Our middle-aged man sleeping in the park was spit upon.

The words we use to validate the pain and suffering that we have endured can go far in determining whether we see ourselves as courageous and resilient or helpless, hopeless, and worthless. The way others come to view our pain and suffering can have an equally powerful effect on our lives. This is most apparent in the lives of those who have been exposed to enduring, inescapable, and traumatizing conditions. Society's recognition of their ordeal can lead to healing and recovery (Raphael, 1991); not acknowledging and validating their ordeal can lead to continued suffering. This appears to be as true for children as it is for adults.

During the 1970s, a number of psychiatrists and psychologists caught a glimpse of the suffering that many Vietnam veterans experienced after their return home. As these veterans began entering hospitals and clinics in different parts of the country, mental health professionals started hearing their stories about the horrible things they witnessed during the war, the traumatizing conditions they were exposed to, and the cold and rejecting way some people treated them when they returned home.

Many of these veterans were suffering serious effects from the trauma they experienced. These effects were reflected behaviorally, psychologically and physiologically in their day-to-day lives. Most professionals, however, didn't connect the symptoms these veterans were displaying to the trauma that they endured in Vietnam. Instead, they saw these veterans as suffering from a mental disorder they themselves had brought on — the result of a flaw from within.

Fortunately, not everyone saw it this way. Bessel van der Kolk (1994) heard their stories and wondered who, if anyone, could be expected to cope with these kinds of horrors. As he listened to their stories he realized how courageous many of these veterans were and, considering the experiences that they endured, how well some of them were actually coping.

When he described to colleagues the symptoms he observed among traumatized Vietnam veterans, child psychiatrists and psychologists noted that the symptoms were very similar to those they were seeing in sexually and physically abused children (van der Kolk, 1994). And yet, in 1982, when van der Kolk asked the director of an inpatient child psychiatry unit whether there were any traumatized children on the unit, the reply was "No." The director said that none of the children were suffering from trauma; they were experiencing conduct disorders, personality disorders, and the like (van der Kolk). The effects of exposure to traumatizing life circumstances was not seen as a major source of children's symptoms.

When van der Kolk (1994) asked the same question ten years later at a meeting that included several directors of child psychiatric units, the reply was, "They all are."

Not all, says van der Kolk (1994), but many. And in years past, we didn't pay much attention to this. I reviewed 60 medical charts of children admitted to a San Diego children's psychiatric facility in the mid-1980s. None of the 60 children in treatment were seen as traumatized. Ten years later, I reviewed 60 additional charts of children admitted to the same facility and found that over 50% of the children were seen as suffering from the effects of trauma. Doctors at the facility told me that this was actually a low estimate; the percentage was probably much higher.

Conclusion

We now recognize that a child's growing up under physically abusive or emotionally abusive conditions, being sexually abused and never being able to talk to anyone about it, being terrified by recurring acts of domestic violence, being removed from home for his or her safety, only to find him- or herself going from one foster home to another, or growing up in an impoverished, inner city war zone can represent enduring, inescapable, and overwhelmingly stressful conditions that can't be altered no matter how hard the child tries. And most of us can understand the struggle of adapting to these conditions. What we have much more difficulty appreciating is the true plight of children with learning disabilities or attention problems. Sure, most of us can appreciate that these children have a hard time of it in school when their needs aren't recognized, but most of us also feel that it's not really that bad. A lot of people didn't do well in school or had run-ins with their teachers. We've all been bruised in some way; we deal with it and go on. Learning disabilities and attention problems, in the great majority of our hearts and minds, do not represent enduring, inescapable, and overwhelmingly stressful conditions.

And yet, after meeting many people with learning disabilities and attention problems, after hearing the stories so many of them tell about what school was like for them, I am sure their experiences were, on occasion, traumatic.

Sometimes their stories are so shocking and alarming that I am convinced if everyone began hearing these stories, things would change in the lives of those who experience these vulnerabilities. They would change quickly, especially for children, since we would realize that it is our lack of awareness of their true plight that has been the major contributor to the stressful conditions they often must contend with. As depicted in chapter 2, however, most of us still don't believe this to be the case.

Chapter 2

The First Day of First Grade: A Positive Experience or Exposure to Inescapable Stress?

Researchers studying the lives of successful adults who overcame childhood adversities have cited instances in which children were able to use successes in one life area to neutralize enduring pain they were feeling in another (Rutter, 1990; Werner & Smith, 1992; Zimrin, 1986). For example, many children growing up in violent situations who were skilled academically and engaging socially were able to use their school experience to neutralize some of the turmoil they experienced at home. From the first day of school, many of these children felt successful and accepted. They were buffered and shielded by their teachers, supported by their friends, and welcomed by their friends' families. They developed a sense of mastery by virtue of their school experience. Career opportunities materialized later down the road. For these children, the first day of first grade may have been a turning point experience. But what about children who experience attention difficulties and learning disabilities? When they begin school, their difficulties, which are likely neurobiologically based, may prevent them from learning and behaving like most other children, even though they desperately want to be like everyone else. They may look like they can do the work, and have intellectual gifts of one form or another, yet, despite their best efforts they don't learn like the vast majority of other children. Our customary response to these children? Try harder, you'll do better. But they won't. For these children, the first day of first grade may be the start of a new source of humiliation from which there is no escape.

Neurobiologically-based difficulties, like attention-deficit/hyperactivity disorder (ADHD) or learning disabilities, have a physical, neurochemical, or neuroanatomical basis (Peschel, Peschel, Howe, & Howe, 1992). Research findings have dispelled the notion that all childhood difficulties are the result of things that parents and caregivers failed to do during the early years of the child's life. Clinicians and educators who identify and treat these types of difficulties try very hard to make parents allies in understanding the nature of the difficulty. They discuss ways that the child can enjoy greater success at home and at school, both today and in the future. Parents are helped to become advocates for their children. In the past, parents were blamed for these childhood difficulties. A few examples of conditions in which researchers have identified neurobiological causes are autism, obsessive-compulsive disorder, Tourette's syndrome, ADHD, and learning disabilities. This chapter focuses on two of the most common neurobiologically-based conditions in childhood: ADHD and learning disabilities.

Children with ADHD

A great many children with ADHD possess a range of impressive talents and intellectual/cognitive capabilities. Often, however, they struggle with daily tasks that most other children can handle with little effort. It's hard to accept that children with multiple talents and capabilities could struggle with things that seem so easy to most others. Why can't these children just sit still, pay attention, and control themselves like everyone else? Why can't they follow the rules, listen to their parents and teachers, and remember to do the simple things requested of them?

It's easy to assume that these children are intentionally not doing what they are asked to do. They can play Nintendo for hours; why can't they sit still in class? They can remember to turn in their homework on Monday; why can't they remember to turn it in on Tuesday?

Since the actions of these children seem so much under their control, and since it's so easy to assume that they could do what we ask if they just tried harder, the natural reaction is to punish them when they don't comply. And if this doesn't work, it's natural to think that all we have to do is increase the severity of the punishments; eventually these children will learn their lesson.

Now imagine for a moment that this behavior really isn't completely under the child's control. The child really can remember directions sometimes and not other times. The child who can play Nintendo for hours really can't sit still in class and pay attention. The punishments have been increasing in severity to eliminate behaviors that the child cannot eliminate. Imagine what this must be like for the child.

Needless to say, the degree of failure and frustration that these children experience and the degree to which they're reprimanded and criticized are enormous. The stress they feel is inescapable. Each day brings more demands that they won't be able to successfully handle, leading to more criticism, failure, and frustration.

The poem below was written by an 11-year-old boy to his mother while he was in a psychiatric hospital. He was hospitalized for out-of-control behavior. While the child was confronting a variety of life stresses at the time, one of his diagnoses was ADHD. His attention difficulties were reported to have caused a great deal of failure and frustration for him in school.

Dear Mom
I am your son who came out as a monster.
I wonder sometimes if you love me or not but I know you do.
I hear imaginary screams in my mind.
I see us as a happy family.
I want us to be a happy family.
I am your son who came out as a monster.

I pretend to hate you sometimes but I love you very much.
I feel a lot of pain when we get in fights but I pretend not to.
I touch God and ask him how to work this out but I get no answer.
I worry I might lose you.
I cry after every argument and think about you.
I am your son who came out as a monster.

I understand why you get so mad and I try to fix that but it's hard.
I dream of running away but I cry when I'm away.
I hope I live with my Dad but I really want to live with you.
I am your son who came out as a monster.

By the time children with ADHD reach ages 12 or 13, even the most skilled parents probably won't be able to prevent them from feeling badly about themselves (Kinsbourne, 1993). One father described his 16-year-old ADHD teenager as "a thoughtful kid who's been beaten up for 16 years as if it's a moral failure, a basic character disorder, questioning his basic worth as a human being" (Kinsbourne).

Researchers tell us that ADHD is the most common behavioral condition diagnosed in children (Amaya-Jackson, Mesco, McGough, & Cantwell, 1992). In addition, we know that ADHD doesn't often exist alone. Frequently, there's an ADHD spectrum of difficulties that include other co-occurring vulnerabilities, the most common being fine motor control problems that affect writing skills, problems making and maintaining friends (despite wanting friends very much), and problems in academic achievement. Regarding this last point, researchers indicate that it is not uncommon for learning disabilities to co-occur with ADHD, although estimates vary on the actual frequency with which this occurs. Estimates range conservatively from 19–26% (Barkley, 1990).

Many children and adults with ADHD dread boredom (Kinsbourne, 1993). Boredom isn't perceived as that feeling of gently dozing off during an uninteresting movie; it's more intense and uncomfortable. The child responds to this very uncomfortable internal state by trying to satisfy it with impulsive stimulation-seeking behaviors. We dramatically underestimate the amount of energy it takes for these children to remain focused during this underlying state.

Children with ADHD also often show great variability in their performance, especially in class (Barkley, 1990), which is particularly painful and confusing to parents, who see their children behaving normally in other situations. Why can't they act this way at school? We don't believe they can't because it looks like they can and because some days they show us they can. Consequences typically follow. The thought of making accommodations for children with ADHD is the last thing on many of our minds, because we don't believe they really need them. Yet, researchers now tell us that these accommodations may be critical if these children are to be successful.

Clare Jones (1994) believes children with ADHD often do better when provided with structure, brevity, and variety or novelty. If we add immediate reinforcement to this, perhaps we can understand why they often can play Nintendo for hours. Nintendo has all four of these elements.

Barkley (1994) states that children with ADHD live moment to moment—the future isn't their concern. "The future is the nemesis of the child with ADHD. It will catch them unprepared." Those who aren't able to plan for the future, he feels, can find themselves in serious trouble in a society that places so much value on future-oriented behavior.

Barkley (1990) also says that children with ADHD have difficulty controlling their behavior. They tend to be governed by the moment and are more likely to respond to rewards that are immediate. Also, the overactivity these children show may be most noticeable during transition times—when they're moving from one situation or activity to another, for example, from lunch period back to the classroom.

Children with ADHD also often have difficulty following rules (Barkley, 1990). Teachers complain that children with ADHD just don't listen. Yet, children with ADHD usually know the rules that they're supposed to follow, and they usually have the skills to follow them. "ADHD is not a problem of knowing what to do. It's a problem of doing what we know" (Barkley, 1994).

We can help children with ADHD and their families if we recognize these characteristics. Given what we're learning about the long-term course of ADHD, spotting it early and responding to the needs of the child, his family, and his school are clearly very important. We now know that ADHD can persist into adolescence and adulthood for many individuals.

Some studies report, for example, that at least 50% of children with ADHD will experience significant residual symptoms as adults. While estimates of ADHD in children range from 3–10%, ADHD in adults may be as high as 5% (Wender, 1987).

Adults with ADHD are more likely than most other adults to act on impulse without considering the consequences of what they're doing. Some of these individuals also tend to be stimulation seekers, possibly because they get bored so quickly. In addition, many have a particularly hard time staying organized and finishing what they start. Most damaging though, is that over the years, many of these individuals have grown distrustful of their talents and capabilities. They've been so damaged by the countless times they failed in school, and the countless other humiliating experiences they've endured in their lives, that some have no idea that these talents and capabilities even exist.

Children with Learning Disabilities

Richard Lavoie (1992a) tells a story about Dan, an adult who had a learning disability his entire life, and who wanted to travel around the country and give presentations to parents and educators about what it feels like to have a learning disability. He approached Mr. Lavoie for some advice. Mr. Lavoie asked if he had any real-life stories he could share with his audiences, making the point that people respond well to stories or anecdotes. Dan said he really couldn't think of any, except for maybe the ear story.

When Dan was 7 years old, he was in first grade and he couldn't read. Dan's dad caught lobsters for a living. His dad's attitude was that everybody in the family had a job, and that Dan's was to do well in school. Everybody had a job to do, and Dan's dad didn't want to hear about anyone not being able to do their job. Dan knew he couldn't read and he was terrified about telling anyone. One day he noticed another little boy in class who also couldn't read, but who nobody ever hassled. This child was deaf. Dan said to himself, "I'll pretend I'm deaf." He began to train himself not to respond to loud noises. When the teacher would call on him in class, he wouldn't answer. He was given hearing tests and flunked them on purpose. Dan said that everything was fine up until one day in June. On that day, Dan's mother and father sat him down and told him that they were very worried about his ears and that tomorrow he would be going into the hospital to have his adenoids removed and to have ear surgery performed. The next day Dan went through ear surgery rather than tell his parents the truth.

Learning disabled adults like Dan, and educators like Lavoie, are helping us to better understand the terror, humiliation, and demoralization that many children with learning disabilities experience during their school years. Imagine how it must feel when you try your best to learn like other children learn, but you can't, and everyone tells you to just try harder. When you still don't get it, it's because you're not trying hard enough. Imagine the potential emotional consequences. The type of stress that the child must endure is inescapable: The child must go to school. Nearly 40% of children with learning disorders will eventually drop out of school (American Psychiatric Association [APA], 1994). This is 1.5 times the average. A study conducted in Los Angeles between 1987 and 1989 showed that 6% of school-aged children had a learning disability. Within the same school district, 41% of the children who committed suicide had a learning disability (Lavoie, 1992b).

Learning disabilities are not the result of an intellectual problem. In fact, many learning disabled children are very talented in nonacademic areas. Learning disabilities are not the result of visual or hearing loss, poor schooling, or a lack of consistent school attendance. Nor are they the result of an emotional problem or poor parenting.

Children with learning disabilities are significantly less able to perform in one or more academic areas, in comparison to how they perform in general intellectual areas. Learning disorders often exist in more than one area; for example, a reading disorder often co-occurs with a mathematics disorder and a disorder of written expression (APA, 1994). Estimates of the frequency of learning disorders range from 2–10%, depending on the definition that's applied. Roughly 5% of students in public school are identified as having a learning disorder. In addition, learning disabilities can persist into adulthood and affect an individual's ability to find employment or get along socially (APA).

According to Lavoie (1992b) learning disabilities represent "a life, language, and learning problem that affects your entire waking day." The same underlying impairment that prevents a child from performing an academic task may also prevent him from completing a chore at home. The poor speller, for example, often can't re-visualize what the word looks like. Not being able to re-visualize, according to Lavoie, is like trying to put together a 500 piece puzzle without a picture of what the completed puzzle should look like. You have no visual image of the finished product in your mind. This same child, who has no visual image of what his spelling word looks like, gets home from school and has to clean his room. He seems to be trying, but isn't doing a very good job. It's possible that this child, who can't re-visualize his spelling word, also doesn't have a very good visual image of what a cleaned room is supposed to look like. It's possible that if he had the completed picture in his mind, he could do a much better job. The point that Lavoie and others are trying to make is that learning disabilities don't stop affecting a student when the school bell rings and he goes home. Children with learning disabilities take their disabilities home with them, and sometimes into their adult lives.

Conclusion

Children exposed to inescapable, enduring, and potentially traumatic surroundings did not bring on the harmful conditions they are growing up under. Likewise, children who experience attention and learning difficulties at school did not choose not to learn to read or pay attention. Regardless of whether childhood risks and adversities are rooted in outside environmental conditions or internal neurobiological ones, the child did not bring them on. And a child may not be able to alter them on his or her own no matter how hard he or she tries. These adverse conditions are also likely to co-occur and endure over the long term, especially in the lives of children and adolescents enrolled in this country's most intensive treatment programs, such as residential and day treatment facilities.

Children whose plight is recognized will receive support and accommodations. Adults will try to alter any known inescapably stressful or traumatizing conditions, rearrange the school environment so that success is possible, and help the child find the right words to understand the pain he's had to endure. We will try to buffer and advocate for these children.

Adults who had to overcome similar adversities in childhood and who are now doing well, relied a great deal on protective influences in their earlier years (Werner & Smith, 1992; Rutter, 1990). Many were buffered by important adults in their lives. They also were able to eventually find the right words to help them legitimize the pain they endured. Many came to recognize a special strength they had, which helped them develop a sense of mastery. And some took advantage of turning point experiences, which helped them see themselves in a new light.

Consider the fate that lies in store for the child whose enduring and inescapably stressful life circumstances aren't known. Or the child whose learning and attention difficulties aren't recognized. We're likely to see this child's emotional and behavioral displays as the result of internal difficulties, or because of emerging character flaws. Adults will be much less protective of children who are viewed this way. These children will likely be defined by their "disturbed" behavior and come to be seen as severely emotionally disturbed, and be treated as such.

Are these children severely emotionally disturbed? What is

normal behavior under these circumstances? Have we ever considered the potential emotional and behavioral effects of exposure to enduring and inescapably stressful or traumatizing conditions? Or the emotional and behavioral consequences of being told that you can learn just like other children if you work harder, when in reality you're working as hard as you can? And have we ever examined the consequences of treating emotional and behavioral displays that arise from a child's efforts to adapt to these conditions as being due to oppositional motives? Or to emerging character flaws?

Deciphering this behavior and understanding the pain beneath it requires that we take a new, fresh look at the nature of the risks and adversities that these children and their families must contend with. Our new look must incorporate what researchers are telling us about the behavioral, emotional, and physiological consequences of exposure to highly stressful and inescapable conditions. We must also recognize that risks co-occur; that environmental and neurobiological risk factors can coexist, making it close to impossible for some children to achieve any semblance of success at home, at school, or on the playground, despite what might appear otherwise.

What can a child, parent, or young adult who is confronting inescapable stress do to improve the quality of his or her life? How can the child who is exposed to multiple risks avoid the expected psychological consequences and go on to be a successful adult? How does the individual who succumbs to multiple risk exposure in childhood and who struggles for years with emotional and behavioral difficulties make use of second- and third-chance opportunities to turn his life around? The answers to these questions are being provided by a new group of experts: the individuals who have actually achieved these accomplishments. The valuable lessons they're teaching us are presented in Part II.

Part II

Beating the Odds

The world breaks everyone, and afterward some are strong at the broken places.

Ernest Hemingway

Chapter 3

On Playing a Poor Hand Well

Protective Influences and Sources of Resilience

In Part I, I discussed childhood risks and adversities — conditions that can originate from either potentially harmful external or internal influences or from combinations of both, and that increase the likelihood that a child and family will suffer harm in some way, sooner or later. Part II focuses on protective influences, or conditions that protect and shield children from potentially harmful risks and adversities. As with risks and adversities, protective influences can originate from external or internal influences or from combinations of both. The right combination of protective influences appears capable of outweighing the effects of exposure to multiple risks and adversities (Werner & Smith, 1992). That is why they are so important to study and to identify.

We all know of protective influences, but might not have described them as such. A close-knit family living in an impoverished and dangerous neighborhood can be protective; children may not feel safe on the street, but they feel safe at home. Even families experiencing great distress can provide protection. In her work with families living in a homeless shelter, Ann Masten cites examples of some homeless mothers who saw their prime necessity as insuring that their child was outside waiting for the school bus each morning (Garmezy, 1992). Parents advocating for a child with special needs, trying to insure that those needs are met, provide protection. So does an older brother or sister helping a younger family member understand a parent's illness, or an aunt or uncle or grandparent helping to raise a child because the child's parents may be unable to do so.

Sometimes protection originates from within the community. A school that offers smaller class sizes, that can address each child's unique learning needs, and highlight each child's special strengths, talents, and interests, is protective. So too are high-quality recreation programs in disadvantaged neighborhoods that children and teenagers go to after school, and stay at for hours. These can be places of safety as well as places where talents are expressed and nurtured and where positive identities are formed. Close and enduring relationships are also protective. Special role models and mentors whom children get to know at school, during after-school activities, or through involvement in youth or church groups are protective. Those who have overcome childhood adversities often identify a special person in their lives—a parent, teacher, coach, counselor, some special person who was always there when needed the most.

Protection can also come from within. Some children, for example, have qualities that draw others toward them in times of need. These children are sparkly. They're great at developing safety nets for themselves, so that when things start to fall apart their lives don't tumble completely out of control. Their safety net is there to catch them. Other children may be strong academically or very skilled socially, so that success in school or on the playground comes pretty easily. In times of need, internal strengths like these can come in very handy.

Protective influences that are more internal in nature, that are related to certain qualities and skills that individuals possess, are frequently referred to as sources of "resilience." Resilience is strength under adversity, the capacity to withstand the effects of exposure to known risk factors and adverse conditions, to "beat the odds," so to speak.

According to James Anthony (1985), "The study of resilience may be among the most important research underway in child development and child psychiatry today." Garmezy (1992), refers to resilience as the nature of nature. He and other dedicated researchers feel that rather than focusing our attention on studying what makes people sick, our most important answers may lie in better understanding how and why some people stay well, despite all odds.

Exposure to Single versus Multiple Risk Factors

Risks and adversities can co-occur. As a result, many children and families have to confront multiple risks and adversities. Overcoming multiple adversities can be much more difficult than overcoming one source of stress or exposure to one specific risk. Researchers have shown that exposure to multiple risk factors or multiple sources of stress significantly increases a child's chances of developing serious problems. We're very concerned, therefore, about the child and family exposed to multiple risk factors, because it's clear that these conditions pose the greatest dangers.

Michael Rutter (1979b) looked at the effects of six different risk factors that result from chronic family adversities: severe marital discord, low socioeconomic status, overcrowding or large family size, paternal criminality, maternal psychiatric disorder, and placement of the child with local authorities (foster placement). He observed that a child exposed to a single risk factor fared as well as children who were not exposed to any. A child exposed to four risk factors increased the likelihood of psychiatric disorder tenfold.

Exposure to multiple risk factors also affects children's early social and intellectual development. Barocas, Seifer, and Sameroff (1985) found this to be the case in a study they conducted of 4-year-old children. Six risk factors were looked at, including injury or illness to the child, maternal hospitalizations, chronicity of maternal mental illness, large family size, parental rigidity, and single parenthood. As the number of risks that the children were exposed to increased, the negative effects increased. Exposure to all six risk factors produced the greatest negative impact on the children's social and intellectual development.

Among children involved in a day treatment program in New York, Gabel, Finn, and Ahmad (1988) found that the presence of four factors in a child's preadmission history strongly predicted the likelihood of the child being referred for inpatient hospitalization or residential treatment following participation in the day treatment program. Two of the factors were related to family or environmental risks: the presence of severe abuse or mistreatment in the child's history, and the presence of substance abuse in a parent. The other two factors were related to the child's behavior and emotional status: the presence of suicidal ideation/behavior and the presence of assaultive and destructive behavior. Children whose preadmission histories did not show the presence of these four factors did well in the program. On the other hand, there was a strong association between a discharge recommendation for inpatient hospitalization or residential placement for children whose histories included these four variables.

As the number of risks that an individual is exposed to increases, the chances of him suffering significant harm also increases. This is true for both children and adults. Garbarino (1995) describes how exposure to multiple risks can impact the quality of our lives. Imagine placing four tennis balls in front of you, says Garbarino, with each tennis ball representing a single risk factor. Your job is to juggle the tennis balls. Most of us can juggle one ball. Some of us can juggle two. Now imagine juggling three balls. A few of us might be able to do this, but not many. Now imagine juggling four balls. Four balls are thrown into the air and what happens? They all fall to the ground. As the risks that we are exposed to mount, there can come a point where it's just no longer possible to function normally. While we might not have been able to juggle three balls, we still caught one or two of them when we tried. Three balls didn't all fall to the ground. When we tried to juggle four balls, however, they all did.

→ Overcoming Exposure to Multiple Risk Factors

In order to better understand resilience and protective influences among children and families growing up under adverse conditions, we're particularly interested in how some individuals successfully overcame exposure to multiple risks.

Werner and Smith (1992) have been following the developmental trajectories of a group of individuals who started their lives with the odds against successful development; they experienced moderate to severe perinatal stress, were born into poverty, were being raised by parents with little formal education, and/or were exposed early on to parental discord or psychiatric illness. Werner and Smith found that one out of three of these high-risk children were adjusting very well as young adults. They were free of serious learning or behavior problems as children and teenagers, had succeeded in school, were handling their home and social lives well, and were eager to take advantage of opportunities that came their way after high school. In contrast, two out of three of the children encountering four or more risk factors by age 2 "did develop serious learning or behavior problems by age 10 or had delinquency records, mental health problems, or pregnancies by the time they were 18 years old" (p. 192).

Among the children who were exposed to multiple risks, Werner and Smith (1992) found three factors that differentiated those who developed well from those who succumbed emotionally.

1. The children who escaped serious harm had personal attributes that produced positive responses from people whom they came in contact with. These children had an active and social temperament, which seemed to help draw others into their lives. They also seemed to gain a sense of pride from their hobbies, interests, and talents. In addition, their teachers at school observed them to be very good problem solvers (Werner, 1995).

2. These children also enjoyed affectional ties with grandparents and older brothers and sisters, who served as parent substitutes. They were buffers, often shielding the children from some of the stresses surrounding them. They also encouraged trust and initiative.

3. The children also enjoyed an external support system, which recognized, valued, and rewarded strengths, talents, and abilities, and also provided the children with a sense of coherence. The added support was gained in many different ways, such as through school experiences, involvement in youth groups, and involvement in church activities.

These factors embrace three sources of protection: protection originating from within the child, as evidenced by personal qualities and attributes; protection originating from within the family, be it a brother or sister or an extended family member, who buffered the child from exposure to surrounding risks; and protection originating from within the community, through an external support system that allowed meaningful and valued relationships to form and which provided the child the opportunity to express special talents, hobbies, or interests (Werner, 1995).

Adults Who Have Turned Their Lives Around

Among the many significant findings that have emerged from Werner and Smith's hallmark study, most striking is the larger-than-anticipated number of individuals who were adapting well as adults, despite having experienced serious coping problems as adolescents.

These individuals took advantage of second-chance opportunities that came their way during periods of transition in their lives (Werner, 1995). They had turning point experiences that significantly improved the quality of their lives. For some, marriage or entry into a long-term committed relationship represented an important turning point. For others, it was the birth of a first child. Some said that establishing themselves in a career or job represented a turning point. Others cited their decision to enroll in community college or to join the armed forces as a way to gain educational or vocational skills. And others cited their involvement in a church or religious community.

Before Werner and Smith published their results, most of us would likely have predicted that these children would continue to struggle most of their lives. The results emphasize the role of turning point experiences and second-chance opportunities that occur throughout the lifespan.

Conclusion

Protective influences exist within children, within families, and within communities (Werner, 1995). Together, these protective influences can outweigh the effects of exposure to a range of childhood risks. The evidence of this is now clear. How to integrate these protective influences into the lives of children, families, and young adults confronting multiple risks is the challenge.

In the next chapter, I present a review of several studies whose findings have helped us learn something new about how childhood adversities are overcome. I'll also review Werner and Smith's landmark study in greater depth, particularly findings related to learning disabled children who are now adapting well as adults. These studies support Lisbeth Schorr's view, expressed in her book, *Within Our Reach: Breaking the Cycle of Disadvantage*: "So much more is known than we are now acting on; the lessons of research and experience combine to explode the myth that nothing works" (Schorr, 1988, p. xxi).

Chapter 4

A Review of the Literature

In this chapter I'll discuss what researchers are learning about individuals who overcame a range of childhood risks and adversities. I'll review findings related to children and adults who overcame traumatic life events, individuals who overcame abusive childhoods, children growing up in dangerous neighborhoods who are doing well, successful adults who were raised by a parent suffering from a serious psychiatric disorder, successful adults who were raised in group homes, successful adults who experienced learning disabilities, and adults with attention difficulties who are adapting well.

What did these individuals need to endure? Where did they find the strength and resilience? Were they shielded and protected in special ways? If so, by whom? What do they see as their turning point experiences, or second-chance opportuni-

ties? These are some of the questions that researchers are finding answers to.

Janoff-Bulman: Overcoming Exposure to Traumatic Life Experiences

Most of us maintain some basic and fundamental core beliefs
about the world and about the place that we occupy in it
(Janoff-Bulman, 1992). These core beliefs allow us to place
trust in others and in ourselves. They provide us a will to go on
when things become very difficult in our lives, and a sense of
hope about the future. Janoff-Bulman has conducted extensive
research on the basic and core beliefs that we maintain and
has helped us to better understand how important they are to
our emotional health and psychological well-being.

These core beliefs comprise three fundamental assumptions:

1. We generally believe that the world is a benevolent and
   good place. While our day-to-day concrete experiences
   might suggest otherwise, most of us nonetheless see the
   world, abstractly speaking, as a good place, where good
   fortune will win out over bad fortune. This underlies our
   sense of hope and our willingness to continue to pursue
   goals. Our day-to-day frustrations, disappointments, and
   failures are not enough to shake our more global and
   abstract view of the world as positive. Most of us believe
   that things will work out in the end.
2. We believe that the world we live in is meaningful.
   Things that happen to us and to others make sense; they
   happen for reasons. We also believe that we can control
   the things that happen to us by how we behave—by how
   just and moral we are. If we do the right things and
   behave the right way, good things will happen to us. If

we do wrong to others, if we behave immorally, we'll be punished.

Many of us are convinced that our planning, effort, and hard work allow us to control what happens to us. It's extremely difficult and troubling for us to believe otherwise, that things can happen to us randomly, in ways that are beyond our ability to control or alter.

3. Our third basic assumption is that we have self-worth. We do good things, we try to help others, we care, we work hard. We have a place in the world, and we've earned it.

These three core assumptions make us feel good. The feelings and emotions that we tie to them are positive and comforting. They may be overgeneralizations, they may be illusions, they may sometimes contradict the reality of real world events—no matter. We still hold onto them, even when shown evidence to the contrary. These core beliefs are too important to us emotionally and psychologically. Some researchers feel, in fact, that they're actually necessary for us to experience psychological well-being and mental health (Taylor, 1989). They allow us to place trust in ourselves and in others, and they give us the incentive to get out and explore and relate to our world.

Few things will alter these basic core beliefs. However, what will alter them, likely even shatter them, is exposure to traumatic life events. Traumatic events that result from the actions of others, particularly those of people whom we know, trust, and depend upon, are particularly likely to shatter our basic assumptions. Such is the case for children who have been traumatized by the actions of close family members or by others whom they looked to for support, security, and a sense of safety.

Janoff-Bulman has studied how both children and adults restore basic core beliefs that were shattered by traumatizing experiences. Through her extensive studies with those who overcame traumatic life events, she found three factors related to the healing process:

1. The individual's ability to tolerate strong and distressing emotions, including the type of physiological arousal that follows exposure to trauma. Individuals who can tolerate these states are more likely to talk about their experiences. This gives them more opportunities to interpret their experience in new ways.

2. The individual's ability to reappraise the experience, that is, to see the experience in a new light. Those with creative talents, who can see things from many different perspectives, might have an advantage here. So too do individuals who derive from their experiences new lessons about life and about themselves, and who can convert this new knowledge into actions that help others.

3. The third factor relates to the support that's available from caring people in the trauma victim's life. A loving support system provides firsthand evidence that the world does care, that the world is meaningful, and that the individual does in fact occupy an important place in it.

Janoff-Bulman feels as well that if our inner core beliefs can be restored to some degree, if we can rebound from extremely hurtful events, we may be better able to cope with future painful experiences. We've learned firsthand that bad things that are beyond our ability to control or to prevent can happen to us. We are now better prepared.

Zimrin: Adults Abused as Children

Child abuse has been described by some as the "critical link" to most problems of youth and later adulthood (Phillips, 1993).

Experts in the field cite an indisputable relationship between child abuse and a range of disorders. In some studies, 90% of individuals exhibiting serious difficulties experienced abusive childhoods. These serious difficulties include alcohol and drug abuse, criminal and gang activities, prostitution, runaway behavior, teen pregnancy, sexual offenses, suicide, and violent crime (Phillips). Yet, many adults who suffered abusive childhoods are now adapting well. What can we learn from them? And how might we be able to use that knowledge to help children suffering the aftereffects of similar conditions? A study conducted by Hanita Zimrin (1986) may help answer these questions. Zimrin identified specific variables that distinguished a group of successfully adjusting adults who had been abused as children from a group of adults who were similarly abused as children, but who were experiencing a high degree of psychosocial pathology.

The study, which was conducted in Israel, followed 28 abused children who had been physically abused between the ages of 3.5 to 5 years by a parent. The children required medical treatment and hospitalization from an injury that was deliberately caused. The control group consisted of children matched in terms of age, sex, parents' country of origin, living conditions and mother's level of education.

Fourteen years later, 19 children were seen as nonsurvivors of their earlier abuse, and 9 were seen as survivors. These findings were based on interviews that looked at scholastic achievement, adjustment to school or work, presence or absence of symptoms of severe emotional problems, and sense of fulfillment or constructive plan for the future. Zimrin also looked at results of military examinations. Acceptance into the army is considered a sign of positive adjustment in Israeli society; rejection is considered a negative indicator.

Several variables distinguished those who were adapting well from those who were not:

- The group of individuals who were adapting well felt a much greater sense of control and influence over their destiny. In fact, they reportedly felt more in control of their destiny than members of the control group did. The nonsurvivors felt fatalistic and submissive: There's nothing I can do to change my destiny, so why fight it?
- Members of the survivor group enjoyed a higher self-image. They were more capable of differentiating between what was attributed to them and what was real. They knew that they didn't cause their abuse. They also found other criteria for evaluating themselves. Members of the nonsurvivor group experienced much the opposite in terms of how they viewed themselves; they often saw themselves as "worthless," "bad," or "stupid."
- Members of the survivor group maintained a sense of hope, which was often expressed in fantasy. One individual said, "I never knew whether I would live tomorrow, but when evening came, I used to stand near the window and imagine the lights of N.Y." There was no such expression of hope for the future among the nonsurvivors; these individuals felt despair.

Situational variables also differentiated the two groups:

- Among members of the survivor group, there was generally a supportive adult involved in their life who proved to be a stable resource over a long period of time. This individual didn't necessarily spend a great deal of time with the child. The important protective influence was his or her stability and availability over time. Most of the survivors mentioned a teacher in school or another person who inspired confidence and encouraged them on. Among the nonsurvivor group, there was generally no mention of a similarly supportive adult.

- • Members of the survivor group also took on the responsibility for helping someone else; for example, protecting and nurturing a sibling in some specific way. Some survivors mentioned the importance of caring for a pet that depended upon them. The nonsurvivors did not mention a similar type of responsibility.

Despite the survivor group's advantages, Zimrin indicates that they still showed problems that required attention. For example, they had difficulty expressing emotions and trusting people. One survivor said, "All my life I surrounded myself with walls . . . I didn't let anybody enter, and didn't reach out to anybody."

What can we learn from this study? Does it offer us information that can be used to help other children who have been exposed to similar abusive experiences? Zimrin's findings show the importance of a trusting, supportive, sincere, and stable relationship over time, as well as the potentially positive influences that come from a special responsibility that one might have for helping others in a meaningful way. Zimrin also stresses the importance of strengthening a child's confidence in both his or her abilities and coping behavior. Her study showed that abused children who are adapting well as adults used external criteria to gain confidence in their worth and capability. For some, achievements at school may have served to neutralize the negative messages at home.

Finally, Zimrin points out that there's great danger in an abused child accepting his fate. She mentions that fighting back and attempting to change the course of events can be very important. Even though the child may not be able to change the existing conditions, the act of fighting back and not accepting the existing conditions as his fate may actually serve to minimize the harmful psychological effects of the abuse.

Baldwin, Baldwin, and Cole: Children Living in Dangerous Neighborhoods

Families who live in high-risk, dangerous neighborhoods are forced to find ways of protecting their children from their surroundings. Research into how these families accomplish this suggests that what may work for them may be entirely inappropriate for families living in more affluent surroundings.

Baldwin, Baldwin, and Cole (1990) studied families living in high-crime, inner-city areas whose children were showing higher-than-anticipated cognitive skills. In many cases, families had limited educational opportunities, low paying jobs, were comprised of single parent households, and were subjected to the effects of minority prejudice. The authors compared these families to families residing in low-risk environments whose children were also showing better-than-anticipated cognitive skills.

- Families living under high-risk conditions imposed more restrictions on their children's freedom, which lowered the child's exposure to risks of the inner city if he or she conformed. The authors point out that since the dangers are real and visible, restrictions can be defended by a parent. In safer communities, these restrictions may seem harsh, unfair, or arbitrary.
- Families living under high-risk conditions were also more vigilant in monitoring their children's compliance. In addition, they placed higher value on children's self control. Among these families, church membership also provided added support for parents' values.
- Both high-risk and low-risk families whose children developed better-than-anticipated cognitive skills placed a high value on responsibility and good judgment.

Baldwin et al. (1990) propose ways to shield children from exposure to the potentially harmful effects of living in dangerous inner-city neighborhoods. Providing well-structured and supervised after-school activities that children enjoy participating in is particularly important; it can offer some control over who children associate with and the dangers they are exposed to. Role models are also important; they can reinforce clear and explicit rules and guidelines as well as family values regarding the importance of education and planning for the future.

Bleuler: Children of Parents with Schizophrenia

Bleuler (1978, 1984) followed 184 children of schizophrenic patients from childhood to adulthood to see how they functioned as adults. The number of children who themselves developed schizophrenia was only 9%. Almost 75% of the entire group were described as healthy functioning adults. Of those who married, 84% have successful marriages. The study cites three important childhood protective factors:

- Opportunities presented themselves for some good parenting from the afflicted parent.
- There was an opportunity to attach to the nonafflicted parent or to a healthy and caring parent substitute.
- There were opportunities to become involved in activities and responsibilities that offered the child a sense of purpose, such as caring for a younger sibling, helping the afflicted parent in some way, or doing special jobs or chores at home.

Prenatal Exposure to Crack Cocaine

The term "crack babies" has been used in recent years to describe a group of infants who were exposed prenatally to crack cocaine. Most of us saw these infants for the first time in television news reports, where they were often pictured quivering and crying. Some people anticipated that these infants would ultimately cost society billions of dollars to help raise and educate, in light of their anticipated wide-ranging neurological and psychological difficulties.

Many of these "crack babies" are now school-age. Interestingly, preliminary follow-up data suggest that they are doing much better than many had earlier thought possible. A group of researchers at the National Association for Prenatal Addiction Research and Education in Chicago followed 300 children who were exposed prenatally to crack for almost seven years. While these children often suffered from a decreased attention span, impulsive behavior, and concentration problems, the researchers believed that the environment these children were being raised in (e.g., poverty, neglect) played a larger role than drug exposure in the womb. When researchers controlled for environmental factors, the children exposed to crack cocaine scored equivalent to children who were not exposed to drugs in the womb on measures of IQ (cited by Kennedy, 1992).

Rutter, Quinton, and Hill: Girls Raised in Group Homes

Rutter, Quinton, and Hill (1990) studied the adult outcomes of children raised in group homes in London. The children were removed from their families in early childhood because of family breakdown. The researchers found that the adults are now adjusting well, and have a marriage partner who is supportive and who does not have significant problems. Having a supportive spouse seemed to neutralize earlier adversity in childhood.

The research team also found that girls who adjusted well also enjoyed positive school experiences while living in their group homes. The researchers felt that these positive school experiences were associated with an increased likelihood of planning when it came to major decisions, such as choosing a marital partner or selecting a work career. Planning was defined as deciding on a marriage partner after knowing the person more than six months; that is, the partner was a positive choice, not chosen because of external pressure or as a means of escape from an intolerable situation. Planning for a work career entailed choosing a job or career that was probable and realistic.

Rutter et al. conclude that successful school experiences are linked to an increased likelihood of planning with respect to choosing a spouse. In turn, choosing a spouse who is supportive and "nondeviant" is associated with a positive marital relationship. And marital support is associated with better social functioning in adult life. Interestingly, they noted that among a matched female control group of non–institutionally-reared women who were also enjoying a positive adult adjustment, planning played no role in their choice of a marital partner. These women likely associated with a healthier peer group and probably had a much greater chance of marrying a well-functioning spouse. In addition, they likely had help, support, and guidance from their families.

The researchers also noted that the effects of positive school experiences had a greater impact on the institutionally-reared women than on the control group. The control group may have had other ways of developing self-esteem, perhaps through rewarding experiences at home. The institutionally-reared women probably had far fewer opportunities for accomplishing things and fewer avenues through which they could develop a sense of mastery.

Some Less Positive Findings

Compared to a matched control group, institutionally-reared women were much more likely to marry or live with a man with significant problems (52% vs. 19%). Also, they were much more likely to become teenage parents than the girls in the female control group (41% vs. 5%, p. < .0001). On the other hand, adult males raised in similar group home settings who were placed there for similar reasons were less likely to marry or live with a woman with significant problems. In addition, compared to institutionally-reared girls, institutionally-reared boys were significantly less likely to become teenage parents.

Individuals with Learning Disabilities Who are Adapting Well

Recent studies have identified various personal qualities, protective influences, and second-chance opportunities that have helped many learning disabled individuals achieve success in adulthood. Three of these research studies will be reviewed here. The first is the Kauai Longitudinal Study, under the direction of Emmy Werner, which began in the 1950s and continues today. Werner and her colleagues are following the life course of 22 children originally diagnosed as learning disabled at age 10. These individuals were last assessed at age 32–34. The vast majority are adapting well.

The second study, conducted by Paul Gerber, Rick Ginsberg, and Henry Reiff, investigated qualities and protective influences operating in the lives of learning disabled adults who have achieved a high level of vocational success. Many of the individuals they studied obtained Ph.D. or M.D. degrees. Some are also earning well over $100,000 per year.

The third investigation, conducted by Nancy Spekman, Roberta Goldberg, and Kenneth Herman, explored factors related to success and life satisfaction among learning disabled young adults. They examined the personal qualities, attitudes, and external supports that distinguished young learning disabled individuals who were adapting successfully from those who were not.

The Kauai Longitudinal Study

Werner (1993) reassessed 22 learning disabled children at age 32 and found that with few exceptions they had grown into responsible adults. They were holding down jobs, enjoying stable marriages, and were not relying on public assistance. Had one made long-range predictions based on how these individuals were functioning at age 18, however, they likely would have been far off the mark. At age 18, for example, many were experiencing significant difficulties that required professional attention. Their futures hardly looked promising, particularly in light of what seemed to be the enduring nature of their struggles. Yet, the great majority turned their lives around and were observed to be adapting well in their early thirties. Werner's findings highlight the importance of a lifespan perspective.

The 22 children (13 boys, 9 girls) were first evaluated for learning disabilities at age 10 by a panel consisting of a pediatrician, a public health nurse, and a psychologist. Criteria for inclusion in the learning disability group required average to above average intellectual functioning, as measured by the Wechsler Intelligence Scale for Children (WISC); a significant delay in reading ability, where reading level was at least one year below grade level; significant WISC scatter, with at least a one standard deviation difference between the verbal and performance IQ scores; and a significant number of errors on the Bender Visual Motor Gestalt Test. Additional criteria included parent and teacher behavior rating scales that showed the child to be persistently distracted, hyperactive, and unable to concentrate. (By today's assessment standards, many of these children might also be seen as having attention difficulties or attention deficit disorder.) Werner indicates that approximately 75% were growing up under conditions of poverty. The 22 children were matched with a nonlearning disabled control group of the same age, gender, racial background, and socioeconomic status.

AGE 17–18

At age 17–18, 90% of the learning disabled children and the children comprising the control group were reassessed. Werner observed that between ages 10 and 18, the learning disabled children had significantly greater contact with specific services and agencies, including the department of education's special services, the police department, and the department of health (either the division of public health nursing or the division of mental health) where they were seen for purposes of diagnosis or therapy. Between the ages of 10 and 18, approximately 80% of the learning disabled children had contact with community agencies, in comparison to only 9% of the control group.

Only 50% of the individuals diagnosed as in need of special help because of learning disabilities actually received some form of assistance during adolescence. Six obtained help in academic skills through either special classes, learning centers, or tutoring, 2 obtained vocational skills training in the Job Corp or rehabilitation programs, 2 received psychotherapy, and 1 received drug therapy.

A comparison of learning disabled teenagers who received special services with untreated learning disabled teenagers revealed very little difference between the two groups. While among the treated group there was a smaller proportion showing low self-esteem and a higher proportion showing more achievement motivation, the majority of the treated and untreated group members weren't very different in most other ways. Members of both groups, for example, weren't very realistic about their vocational and educational plans after graduation from high school, enjoyed only poor to fair family and social lives, and were limited in their participation in activities in their senior year in high school. Both groups also scored significantly lower on measures of personal adequacy and self-assurance. In addition, measures of locus of control indicated that both treated and untreated group members believed more strongly than controls that they couldn't influence their fate by their own actions.

Only 25% of the learning disabled individuals at age 17–18 had improved their lives. The few who did attributed their improvement to the sustained help of family members, friends, or elder mentors, who they felt bolstered their self-esteem. Most considered intervention by counselors, mental health professionals, and special educators not to be of much help.

AGE 32–34

The groups were reassessed at age 32–34. Information was gathered on each individual's work, family, and social life, and their existing state of health. Werner found that the life course of most had improved considerably. Less than 10% had criminal records or persistent mental health problems. Their marriage, divorce, and employment rates were similar to those of the control group. Also, 40% of the learning disabled individuals had obtained additional schooling from junior colleges. Twenty-five percent still worried about their work, however, and reported stress-related problems at a rate twice as high as the controls. While 2 out of 13 males and 2 out of 9 females had persistent problems, on closer examination it was found that each of these individuals also had significantly more risk factors present in their earlier lives. For example, the two men grew up in homes where parents suffered from alcoholism.

By age 32–34, roughly 75% of the learning disabled individuals were judged to have made a successful adaptation to the demands of work, family, and social life. Among the control group, approximately 80% were judged to be adapting successfully.

PROTECTIVE INFLUENCES

How did the learning disabled individuals turn their lives around? What were the protective influences in their lives? What were their turning points? Werner found great similarity between the protective influences that worked for the learning disabled individuals and those that have been found to help other individuals who overcame entirely different earlier life adversities. Many of the learning disabled individuals, for example, had the type of temperament that allowed them to draw in positive social responses from significant individuals, like parents and teachers. Many also had realistic educational and vocational plans and an important responsibility of some kind that was seen as very helpful to others. Werner indicates that many also had faith that they could overcome the odds against them.

In addition, supportive adults often played an important role in the earlier lives of the learning disabled individuals. Grandparents, elder mentors, youth leaders, or members of the individual's church, for example, acted as a kind of gatekeeper to the future. They were trusted and they in turn fostered trust and faith.

According to Werner, there were also identifiable second-chance opportunities that often opened up for the learning disabled individuals. These opportunities frequently occurred during a life transition period, and seemed to nurture a new sense of confidence and competence. For some, community colleges provided an important second-chance opportunity and proved to be a strong force for positive change in their lives. For others, involvement in the armed services was an important turning point; the military provided opportunities to acquire additional educational and vocational skills. Others found that involvement in a church or religious community offered a sense of meaning to their lives and was a significant force for positive change.

THE PROMOTION OF SELF-ESTEEM

Werner feels that the promotion of self-esteem and self-efficacy is probably the key to any effective intervention program for learning disabled youth, or for that matter, any high-risk individual. Her findings reveal that self-esteem could be derived from many sources, including hobbies, participation in cooperative groups, and from having jobs and responsibilities that others see as particularly valuable and helpful. Most of the learning disabled individuals in the Kauai study enjoyed hobbies and activities unrelated to school, which provided solace when things weren't going well in their lives, especially at school. As teenagers, they frequently took part in activities that allowed them to be part of a cooperative experience with others. Many were involved in Boys and Girls Clubs, the YMCA, or 4H Clubs. Also, at some point, usually in middle childhood and adolescence, the learning disabled youths who later adapted well were often asked to take on a special job or responsibility that required they help out a family member, neighbor, or someone in the community. This was seen as important and valuable work; it was work that was helping others in a meaningful way. Researchers sometimes use the term "required helpfulness" (Rachman, 1979) to describe the benefits derived from actions that lend a helping hand to others in times of need.

Most of all, self-esteem was promoted through supportive relationships. All of the learning disabled individuals who are doing well had at least one person in their lives who accepted them unconditionally, regardless of their handicaps or scattered school performance.

IMPLICATIONS
Given the presence of a chain of protective influences in the lives of vulnerable children and families, the odds of overcoming a variety of different adverse life circumstances seem to increase significantly. Werner feels that it is the job of professionals and caretakers to help put this chain of protective influences in place. These protective influences would include the informal sources of support and protection that involve the participation of older siblings, grandparents, elder mentors, neighbors, youth group leaders, or members of one's church. Among their contributions, they can provide the child with a repertoire of new problem-solving skills and can increase his or

her sense of self-efficacy. Research on the lives of individuals who have overcome earlier childhood adversities has repeatedly shown the positive value that these sources of support play.

Werner notes that care would optimally involve a cooperative effort that includes the involvement of individuals close to the child as well as professionals from different disciplines. Informal sources of support that can take effect early and that can stay in place for a long time would be an integral part of the care plan. For learning disabled children, special teachers and tutors would also play an important role, by helping them improve their academic skills during the first three grades. As these children grow older, vocational counselors would play an important role by helping them set realistic and achievable vocational and career goals. Knowing the frequency with which learning disabled adults sought additional education through community colleges, community college instructors would become key people, welcoming the learning disabled adults back to school, knowing that returning to school could represent an important second-chance opportunity and a potential turning point experience in their lives.

Gerber, Ginsberg, and Reiff: Adults with Learning Disabilities Who Have Achieved Vocational Success

While we know there are learning disabled adults who have achieved a high level of vocational success, up until recently they have not received much attention. Gerber, Ginsberg, and Reiff (1990) conducted a study designed to learn more about these adults. In selecting learning disabled individuals for their study, the authors used a nomination process, whereby various national organizations that work with and advocate for those with learning disabilities were asked to select potential candidates. Candidates were then screened by the project coordinator via structured 40–50-minute phone interviews. The interview addressed matters pertaining to occupation, job satisfaction, and severity of the candidate's learning disability. Potential candidates were placed into one of two groups: a high success group and a moderate success group. Success was defined across five variables: income level, job classification, education level, prominence in one's field, and job satisfaction. Each candidate was rated as either high, moderate, or low in each of the five areas by a panel of five experts in the field of learning disabilities. Placement in the high success group required a high rating in four of the five areas, and no low rating. Placement in the moderate success group required a majority of moderate ratings in each of the five areas, and no more than one low rating. The investigators then matched individuals from the high and moderate groups with one another. They controlled for age (within five years), gender, race, severity of disability, the specific nature of the learning disability, mother's and father's occupations, and parents' socioeconomic status.

The final sample was comprised of 71 individuals, 46 in the high success group, and 25 in the moderate success group. The average age of the high success group was 45.5, with ages ranging from 29 to 67. Their average yearly income ranged from $30,000 to more than $100,000. Thirty-six members of this group had earned Ph.D.s or M.D.s. The average age of members of the moderate success group was 44, with ages ranging from 34 to 59. Their average yearly salary was between $40,000 and $50,000. Sixteen had earned M.A. degrees and 3 had earned Ph.D. or M.D. degrees.

Each participant was then interviewed on tape for an average of 4.5 hours. Interviews covered nine categories: success, vocation, education, family, social issues, emotional issues, the nature of the learning disability, daily living, and recommendations for children currently experiencing learning disabilities.

Information from the interviews was then analyzed for themes and subthemes. Project staff and consultants assisted in the analysis to test the validity of the themes discerned from the interviews.

FINDINGS

An overriding theme among both groups was a quest to gain control over one's life. This pursuit of control was characterized by identifiable personal qualities and skills, including the strong desire to succeed and the capacity to set and reach goals. In addition, members of both groups showed the capacity to reframe their disability experience in a more positive way and possessed helpful coping mechanisms for dealing with stresses. Members of both groups also enjoyed a goodness of fit between their particular skills and the situations they worked in; work-related demands matched up well with their skills, allowing them to experience success on the job. Members of both groups also enjoyed support from important persons in their lives.

While these personal qualities and skills were identifiable among both the high and moderate success groups, important differences were observed in the degree to which they existed. The following list outlines these differences.

- *Quest for personal control.* While members of both groups sought personal control over their lives, members of the high success group achieved this to a much greater degree — they sought more control and realized more control. Gerber et al. note that many members of the moderate success group sought control primarily to cover up their disability as a form of self-protection rather than to move ahead. While the fear of being found out was also observed in the high success group, it was more prominent in the moderate success group.
- *Desire to succeed.* The desire to get ahead was also stronger among members of the high success group. One

member said, "Just tell me I can't do something, and I'll do it." While members of the moderate success group also showed a desire to get ahead, Gerber et al. indicate that it wasn't nearly as strong.

- *Setting and achieving goals.* The high success group consciously set goals for themselves, and sometimes these goals were lofty. These individuals needed to succeed and were anxious about failure. Members of the moderate group had fewer clear goals and less ambitious aspirations.
- *Reframing one's learning disability.* Members of both groups were able to reframe their learning disability experiences in a more positive light. They differed, however, in the degree to which they were able to do this. Members of the high success group were more accepting of their learning disability, whereas members of the moderate success group seemed to have some trouble accepting it.
- *Persistence.* High success group members were also distinguishable by their high level of persistence. To be persistent was a way of life for them. They worked extremely hard and often felt passionate about their work. The moderate group was also very persistent; however, members were not as tenacious as the high success group. Members of the high success group were also seen as more resilient. They were more driven and took more risks.
- *Goodness of fit.* Members of both groups enjoyed a goodness of fit between their particular skills and qualities and the demands posed by their environments. Members of the high success group, however, often *created* a goodness of fit that allowed them to be their own boss or to have the flexibility to make significant decisions about their work. Even as children, many of these highly successful individuals sought out or created environments where they could be both successful and comfortable.
- *Learned creativity.* Members of the high success group also possessed what the authors described as "learned cre-

ativity." Learned creativity refers to the strategies that individuals use to perform tasks that they aren't able to do successfully because of a disability. Members of the high success group didn't just cope with their disability, they creatively excelled. They used their creative talents to develop alternative ways of handling tasks and solving problems. Some members of the high success group also developed very sharp anticipatory skills; they would recognize in advance when something was coming their way that could pose difficulties and plan ahead on how to handle the situation successfully.

* *Supportive relationships.* Although members of both groups surrounded themselves with supportive individuals, members of the high success group seemed to utilize support more to their advantage. They were more willing to seek it out and accept it when offered. This may relate to their greater acceptance of their disability.

IMPLICATIONS

Gerber et al. feel that the qualities and skills found among very successful learning disabled adults can be enhanced in others. The reframing of one's learning disability experiences in a more positive light appears to be particularly important. Recognition of the learning disability is not enough; acceptance and understanding must follow. Constructive action is then possible.

Individuals who have successfully overcome other adverse conditions also go through a similar reframing process. It seems to be a broad-based protective mechanism that assists individuals in overcoming a variety of early childhood adversities. Without this mechanism, an individual may develop learned helplessness; with it, he or she may develop learned creativity.

Participants in general felt that school had little connection to their success. Participants in this study attended school before the passage of federal law 94-142, which paved the way for school-based remedial services to learning disabled students. The question remains to be answered whether similarly successful adults in the future, who received remedial services at school, will attribute their success to these school experiences.

Spekman, Goldberg, and Herman: Factors Related to Success in Young Adults with Learning Disabilities

Spekman, Goldberg, and Herman (1992) wanted to better understand why some adults who experienced learning disabilities as children were adapting well and why others were not. The authors recontacted 50 young adults between the ages of 18 and 25 who were former students at the Marianne Frostig Center of Educational Therapy in Pasadena, California. All had spent at least one academic year at the Frostig Center, and each received an initial diagnosis of learning disability. There was no initial diagnosis of severe emotional disturbance. All had a verbal or performance IQ of 85 or above, and there were no uncorrected sensory deficits or locomotor problems. The researchers gathered information via semistructured interviews, lasting from 1 to 4 hours. They also conducted interviews with the parents, administered brief cognitive and academic screenings, and reviewed previous case records. Three independent raters analyzed the interview summaries and classified the participants into two groups, successful or unsuccessful.

Criteria for inclusion into the successful group included the following: demonstration of age-appropriate activities and endeavors (such as being employed or enrolled in school or in a vocational program), being involved with peers and family members, and participating in leisure and social activities; self-ratings that reflected a general satisfaction with one's life; and descriptions of school, employment, and social activities that were consistent with self-perceptions, capabilities, and aspirations. Criteria for inclusion in the unsuccessful group included:

considerable difficulty with age-appropriate activities; often
feeling dissatisfied with one's life, as revealed through self-
ratings; and/or descriptions of activities, experiences, or aspirations that did not match up with one's self-perceptions.

Of the 50 participants, 29 (58%) were placed in the successful group, and 21 (42%) were placed in the unsuccessful group.
More than 80% were Caucasian and 60% were male. The
two groups did not differ significantly with respect to family
socioeconomic background, race, and gender.

Both groups achieved similar performance IQ and full scale
IQ scores at the time of their admission to the Frostig Center.
The successful group did score higher on the verbal IQ (101.5)
than the unsuccessful group (92.8), but the authors point out
that on follow-up, there were members of the unsuccessful
group with strong verbal abilities, and members of the successful group with a low verbal IQ. Also, when tested as adults
during the follow-up phase, the participants' scores on verbal
and performance IQ tasks did not significantly differentiate
the groups. The authors maintain that the relationship between IQ and successful outcome remains unclear.

At the time of admission to the Frostig Center, similar pro-
portions of additional diagnoses were found in the two groups.
Co-occurring diagnostic classifications included organic, hy-
perkinetic, and mild to moderate emotional problems. Among
the successful group, 32.1% had an additional diagnosis of
organic, compared to 40% for the unsuccessful group; 3.6% of
the successful group had an additional diagnosis of hyperki-
netic, compared to 5% of the unsuccessful group; and 68% of
the successful group had an additional diagnosis of mild-to-
moderate emotional problems, compared to 85% of the unsuccessful group.

FINDINGS

Spekman et al. found three themes, working in association
with one another, among members of the successful group: a

realistic adaptation to life events, appropriate goal setting and goal directedness, and the use of effective support systems. The three themes were absent in the unsuccessful group. The following discussion explores these three themes in greater depth.

The first theme, realistic adaptation to life events, was characterized by a self-awareness and acceptance of one's disability, the capacity to act proactively, the capacity to persevere, and the ability to cope with stressful situations.

- *Self-awareness and acceptance.* Members of the successful group were aware of their disability; they accepted it and understood it. The disability did not define their identity. They were also able to recognize their strengths and maintain a realistic adaptation to life events. Members of the unsuccessful group tended to deny their difficulties; perhaps because of this they were openly critical of those who tried to help them. They also were often unable to recognize that it was possible to alter a situation and that there might be multiple solutions to problems.
- *Proactive approach toward decision making.* Members of the successful group felt that they had the power to make positive changes in order to control their own destiny. Members of the unsuccessful group tended to be more passive and avoidant.
- *Perseverance.* Members of the successful group showed a high degree of perseverance. Difficulties that they encountered were more likely to be viewed as learning experiences. This group showed a willingness to keep at it, despite the adversities they confronted. Members of the unsuccessful group were more likely to externalize blame for their difficulties, to give up more easily, and to be overwhelmed by adversities.
- *Ability to cope with stressful situations.* Members of the successful group showed greater coping strategies and

were more capable of reducing the stress in their lives. Members of the unsuccessful group often seemed unable to reduce their stress. The successful group also showed greater emotional stability and were generally able to express a positive outlook. They enjoyed good peer relationships and were active socially.

The second overall theme, goal setting and goal directedness, is evidenced by members of the successful group setting goals that were realistic and achievable, and that seemed to give some meaning and direction to their lives. Members of the unsuccessful group seemed to lack goals and a sense of direction. When goals were discussed, they tended to be grandiose and unrealistic. The authors note that more than 40% of the unsuccessful group gave no evidence of having future educational or employment plans.

Members of the successful group utilized an effective support system; they identified significant individuals in their lives who encouraged and guided them. Some identified family members. Others identified a teacher, tutor, or mentor. These relationships lasted a long time and were especially helpful during transition periods. They were also able to seek out and find support as their interests changed and as they passed through different developmental phases. While members of the unsuccessful group also had access to relationships with tutors and counselors after they left the Frostig Center, the relationships they formed were often short-term, reactive, and crisis-oriented.

The authors note that the richest source of information came from personal interviews with each of the participants. Certain parallel themes emerged that held true for members of both the successful and unsuccessful groups:

- Learning disabilities represented an ongoing condition, regardless of the amount of intervention that was received. Some common areas of persisting struggle included academic tasks, organizational problems, memory problems, spatial orientation difficulties, and having to work harder and longer than one's peers. Several participants also said they lost jobs because of the persisting impact of their learning disabilities.

- All participants experienced additional life stressors. Sometimes, added stress came from having to manage employment-related difficulties.

- There was a sense of postponement among members of the successful group regarding achieving financial independence, as well as in terms of establishing long-term relationships. Some of the participants said they were distancing themselves from others for fear that others would "find out" about their disability. Regarding their continued dependence on family: Only 1 out of the 50 participants was found to be financially independent. Continued family dependence was linked to such factors as prolonged periods in school, low-paying jobs, and problems in handling money. Spekman et al. indicate that most of the participants did not have any immediate plans to alter their living situation.

Other findings revealed that although reading level did not discriminate between the two groups, math level did. The successful group appeared more skilled in handling math-related tasks. The authors speculate that the unsuccessful group members may not have achieved a mathematics skill level necessary for handling personal affairs, such as finances or shopping. In addition, their math skills may have been too low for even beginning level jobs (such as retail jobs).

Members of both groups described added stresses in their lives that coexisted with their learning disabilities. The authors note however that traumatic events such as parent divorce or death did not occur with greater frequency among members of the unsuccessful group. Thus, these risk factors seemed unrelated to their less successful outcome.

For young adults with learning disabilities, the authors suggest that the timing of age-appropriate behavior may have to be modified. They feel that these young adults may need guidance and resources for longer periods of time than might have been realized. This is not to say, however, that these individuals won't enjoy a better adjustment in the future. The authors cite Werner's (1993) findings, for example, which showed a larger-than-anticipated number of adults who were functioning well, despite experiencing adjustment difficulties as teenagers.

IMPLICATIONS
Spekman et al. conclude that we need to help the child with learning disabilities understand the disability in a realistic way so that it does not define his or her personal identity. Also, we should be assessing internal and external protective factors that can counteract prevailing risk factors. In addition, tutors and teachers need to be aware of their potential impact as mentors to the learning disabled child.

This study highlights the importance of a lifespan perspective when addressing the needs of the child with learning disabilities. Findings suggest that we focus on preparing the learning disabled individual for life in the real world and provide him with opportunities for meaningful employment. Findings also suggest that we remain sensitive to the learning disabled individual's needs after high school, keeping in mind that services and support may be necessary beyond the school years.

Adults with Attention Difficulties Who Are Adapting Well

In our quest for answers about how individuals overcome life's adversities, Norman Garmezy (1992) reminds us that there is much that can be learned from an "n of 1." Gabrielle Weiss and Lily Trokenberg-Hechtman (1993), who have been following the adult developmental trajectories of children with attention difficulties, tell the story of Ian Murray. Originally diagnosed with attention difficulties over 20 years ago, Ian is now 27 and doing well. Currently, he works in a children's residential treatment center, where he is valued for his ability to understand and reach the children he works with. Ian plans to finish his college studies and apply to medical school.

As a child, Ian was hyperactive, learning disabled, and noncompliant. During his teenage years, some antisocial behavior was also evident. The authors cite Ian's personality strengths, unusual insight, and self-awareness as possible factors that helped him to eventually adapt well as an adult.

At the request of the authors, Ian took a look back and documented what it was like for him to grow up with ADHD and learning difficulties. He wrote about the things that helped and the things that hurt. Recognizing Ian's expressive talents, Weiss and Trokenberg-Hechtman wanted him to share his thoughts and feelings with the rest of us, so that we all might learn from his experiences. A selection of Ian's reminiscences follow.

> My dignity and self-esteem rested on my ability to conceal from anyone that there was anything wrong with me. (p. 302)

> The recognition of not fitting in and the emergence of a sense of pessimism started to take shape in Grade 1. (p. 320)

> I was never told about what the various tests were supposed to measure and whether I had done all right or failed. I was never left with a sense of hope, or a feeling of any clinician's real interest in being a partner with me to help me grow and learn. Rather the mystification of what was wrong with me was reinforced with each new test, indicating to me that the problem was not yet clear. (p. 320)

> [Sneaking into his sister's room one day, Ian found] *Catcher in the Rye* by Salinger; thumbing through it I realize it's about a boy in trouble. I can't pass it up. I keep going back to it, wonder-

ing if I might be able to read it. I take the book back to my room. Sentence by sentence, page by page, a new world opens up to me. This is what I have been waiting for. It's a struggle, but the payoff is enormous. Emotionally, the book compels me to pay attention and not lose track. I go over it again and again. I discover that I can read. (p. 313)

Mrs. Wilson was the best teacher I ever had. Although strict, she was encouraging and supportive. She understood what I could and couldn't do. I was never thrown out of class; instead, she kept me after school and I would help her clean up, set things up for the next day. She got to know me and sensed that I wanted to please, that I craved for sincere, positive feedback. (p. 313)

During his teenage years, Ian says that he had other ideals and values to aspire to, which were outside the mainstream of authority or convention. "This in no small way allowed me to understand that I could learn" (p. 321). During this time in his life, Ian found himself becoming more introspective and better able to assess the impact that he had upon those around him. He also became better able to compensate for what he refers to as a wandering mind. Ian learned how to mirror the appropriate expressions and gestures while conversing with others so that he at least could look as though he was paying attention; though, in actuality, his mind may have been wandering off to other thoughts.

SOURCES OF RESILIENCE AMONG INDIVIDUALS WITH ADHD

In searching for possible sources of resilience among young adults who struggled with ADHD throughout their lives, Hechtman (1991) notes that some of the most positive outcomes were among individuals who possessed special skills and abilities. She also notes the important role that a caring relationship played in their lives, someone who always believed in them, whether it be a parent, teacher or coach. Interestingly, these same sources of resilience and protection often appear in the lives of those who overcame very different childhood adversities. As noted, for example, Zimrin (1986) found these factors to be present in the lives of successful adults who were abused as children.

Conclusion

There are a growing number of researchers who feel that there are important lessons to be learned from those who have overcome adverse childhood experiences. In the preceding discussion I have reviewed the work of some of these researchers. In Part III, which follows, we begin the process of passing on these lessons. Werner and Rutter, two of the leading researchers in the field of human resilience, define a series of broad-based protective influences that often run through the lives of individuals who have overcome childhood adversities. These protective influences synthesize some of their research findings, as well as the findings of others. This is only a beginning. New research findings are sure to lead to more identifiable protective influences in the future.

Part III

Changing the Odds

It is a strange and tragic paradox that confidence in our collective ability to alter the destinies of vulnerable children has hit rock bottom just as scientific understanding of the processes of human development and the rich evidence of success in helping such children have reached a new high.

Lisbeth Schorr

Chapter 5

Finding the Words

The difference between the right word and a word is like the difference between lightning and a lightning bug.

Mark Twain

A fifth grade student at Lake Elementary School in Oceanside, California, learned one day that he had leukemia and that he might die. What was particularly upsetting to the child, however, was one of the anticipated side effects from the chemotherapy treatment he was about to start: He was going to lose his hair — it might fall out in school, around his friends, and in two weeks his hair might all be gone. His friends at school and his teacher, Jim Alter, found out about this. They didn't want him to feel embarrassed or different, so they all decided to shave their heads. The thirteen fifth graders, the teacher, and the child with leukemia all went to a local barber shop and had their heads shaved. The story appeared in the *San Diego Union* (Silvern, 1994) the following day, accompanied by a picture of the fourteen children with their teacher, standing close to one another, all bald, and all smiling for the camera. It's impossible to tell which child has leukemia. The children named themselves the "Bald Eagles."

Researchers tell us that if we can learn to see risks and adversities in a new way, we may be able to dramatically influence their potentially negative, or in some cases devastating, impact on our lives. This is true for both children and adults. The process of learning to see adversities in a new light requires that we find the words and the language to legitimize and validate the pain we've endured, or perhaps are still enduring. Having the right words can literally mean the difference between coming to define oneself as courageous and resilient or worthless, helpless, and hopeless. The child with leukemia learned to see the hardship he was confronting in a new way, and this significantly changed the quality of his life.*

While the story of the "Bald Eagles" is, in part, about how a child with leukemia "beat the odds," it is also a story about how the child's friends and teacher changed them. The fact is, we can change the odds in an individual's life simply by how we choose to view the adversities that individual is confronting. The life course of an individual is greatly affected by whether or not society recognizes the suffering he or she has endured. Society's recognition aides in healing and recovery (Raphael, 1991). Not acknowledging and validating the individual's ordeal, on the other hand, can lead to continued suffering. This has enormous implications for healthy children growing up in unhealthy surroundings.

Healthy Children Growing Up in Disturbed Worlds

Lenore Terr (1990) studies the lives of children who have been traumatized, who know the feeling of terror. She classifies a

*I recently spoke to Jim Alter, the teacher who shaved his head, and found out that this child with leukemia has been free of symptoms for some time now—he is healthy and doing well.

one-time traumatizing experience as a "type I" trauma. Repeated traumatizing experiences are "type II" traumas—ones that happen over and over again and that are inescapable. The child's job is to adapt. Exposure to violent relationships at home, being abused physically, sexually, or emotionally by a family member, or growing up in a very violent and dangerous neighborhood are all conditions that researchers cite as potential sources of type II traumas.

We have learned that healthy children are exposed to these conditions in greater numbers than anyone ever imagined. Many of these children no longer see themselves as healthy, but instead as deserving of what is happening to them. This happens, as Terr (1990) points out, because children lack perspective.

Unless we help these children learn to see their lives differently, the potential consequence is a sense of hopelessness, helplessness, and despair. Over time, these children may come to feel futureless. Garbarino (1994) refers to this as terminal - thinking. Like the fifth-grade child with leukemia, the healthy child growing up in unhealthy surroundings needs loving individuals who can communicate an understanding of what he's feeling and what he's living through in a way that leaves no doubt in his or her mind. We legitimize and validate the child's pain when we do this; the child then learns to see his or her adversities in a new light. We've changed the odds.

Immunizing Children against Feelings of Hopelessness, Helplessness, and Despair

Researchers are now showing us how to prevent hopeless, helpless, and depressed feelings from occurring, and how to eliminate them if they have already taken hold of our lives. Researchers are especially knowledgeable about how to accomplish this in childhood. Children can be taught that they have a choice in how to view difficult or even traumatic events

occurring in their lives. They can learn to stop blaming themselves for stressful events that are beyond their ability to control and to generate new and novel ways of solving problems.

The Penn Prevention Model

Martin Seligman (1995) and his associates developed the Penn
Prevention Model to teach these skills to children, especially
to children who are at risk for serious depressive symptoms
in the future. The prevention project incorporates strategies
designed to teach children how to be more flexible and accu-
rate in their thinking and how to solve problems they face.
The program is school-based, with lesson plans designed by
Seligman and his associates. Lessons are taught in small groups
by trained assistants.

The Penn Prevention Model initially targeted 70 fifth- and
sixth-grade children in a school district outside of Philadelphia
who were found to be at risk for depression. A matched control
group from another school district was formed so that results
of the program could be evaluated against a group of similarly
at-risk children who did not receive the intervention. Before
the intervention program began, 24% of the children in both
groups were showing moderate to severe depressive symptoms.
Immediately after the program ended, 13% of the intervention
group were showing similar levels of depression, compared to
23% of the control group. Two years after the program ended,
22% of the intervention group reported moderate to severe
depression, while 44% of the control group reported these
symptoms.

A significant number of children who participated in the
Penn Prevention Project learned that they had control over
how they viewed themselves and the problems that they confronted. They learned not to attribute problems to permanent
causes, how to catch themselves when they began drawing
unfair and inaccurate conclusions about themselves and the

events that troubled them, and what options were available for responding to a problem in their lives. They also learned how not to think in catastrophic ways, how not to think of the worst possible explanation for particular problems; they learned that problems are solvable and their response to them, controllable. These skills helped develop a sense of mastery in these children, which in turn protected them from feeling helpless, hopeless, and depressed.

The Penn Prevention Program has been expanded to other school districts in Pennsylvania. The program is now being offered to children in the inner city of Philadelphia. In an effort to reach many more children, Seligman and his colleagues are now training teachers and parents to carry out the same interventions used in the Penn Prevention Project.

Telling Stories in Ways that Heal

Stories are Beings. You invite them to live with you. They'll teach you what they know in return for being a good host. When they're ready to move on, they'll let you know. Then you pass them on to someone else.

A Cree Storyteller

The stories we tell about each other and ourselves can be healing. They help us to validate painful experiences that we have endured and to withstand difficult roads that might lie ahead. But the stories we tell can also be harmful. Arlan Neskahi (1995), a training specialist for the Western Regional Center in Portland, Oregon, shares the following excerpt from a report by J. D. C. Atkins, U.S. Commissioner of Indian Affairs from 1885 to 1888:

The instruction of Indians in the vernacular (that is, in Indian language) is not only of no use to them, but is detrimental to the cause of their education and civilization, and it will not be permitted in any Indian school over which the government has any control . . . This (English) language, which is good enough for the white man and a black man, ought to be good enough for the red man. It is also believed that teaching an Indian youth in his own barbarous dialect is a positive detriment to him. The first step to be taken toward civilization, toward teaching the Indians the mischief and folly of continuing their barbarous practices, is to teach them the English language.

The meaning that we ascribe to things that have occurred in our lives or in the lives of others determines the kinds of stories we will tell. And we may have to retell stories of things that have caused us harm, or of assumptions and beliefs about us that are wrong. These stories may need to be retold with words that legitimize, validate, and empower us.

Some family therapists now specialize in approaches that help individuals retell personal stories in ways that heal. Michael White and David Epston (1990) are two family therapists who are leading the way. They refer to their work as narrative therapy.

In their work with individuals and with families, White and Epston witnessed the ways in which individuals were affected by the particular meaning they ascribed to difficult life circumstances. The stories their clients told were often oppressive in tone. They defined themselves around these "problem saturated stories" (White & Epston, 1990), and had a very difficult time seeing alternative interpretations of difficult and troubling experiences and life events.

White and Epston began helping these individuals retell their personal stories in new ways. These new, alternative stories are liberating and empowering in their tone. They highlight one's courage and free one from immobilizing feelings of self-blame. Particular problems no longer define one's identity or the nature of one's relationships. Individuals learn to externalize their particular problems, to see them from a distance.

Therapists, in general, rely a great deal on the spoken word to help individuals see their world in new, more liberating ways. White and Epston tell us, however, that the spoken word represents only one way of reauthoring personal stories. Another is through the written word. In our culture, the written word seems to hold special importance. According to White and Epston (1990), there's something official and believable when we see things in writing: "I'll believe it when I see it in writing" or "make sure you get it in writing."

Realizing the authenticity that the written word carries, narrative therapists help individuals to retell their stories in writing. Some therapists also communicate in writing to their clients, using language and text that help to open up new avenues of interpretation for life events that were previously told with words that were limiting and devaluing.

Not long ago, I had the opportunity to communicate in writing to a mother of a 16-year-old teenager with attention deficit disorder and learning disabilities whose identity was being negatively influenced by his frustrating school experiences (Katz, 1994). He was beginning to define himself in negative and devaluing ways. The mother of the teenager wrote a letter to the editor of a national newsletter sponsored by CH.A.D.D. (Children and Adults with Attention Deficit Disorder), requesting help for her son. The parent's letter and my reply are reprinted here.*

To: Ask CH.A.D.D. Q and A Column
From: A Concerned Parent

My 16-year-old was diagnosed with ADD when he was a little boy. He also has learning disabilities in reading and math, and school has been a constant struggle. Even so, I

*Thanks to the Board of Directors of CH.A.D.D. and the editorial staff of their national newsletter for permitting me to reprint the letter.

*have received very few comments about behavior problems
from his teachers over the years. While Kurt is miserable in
the classroom (he says that the school day is "about 20 hours
long") he shines in music and theater, and has many good
friends. People who hear him play trumpet in the pep band
or see him act in plays (he is very clever) assume he will be a
big hit in life. However, his grades are mostly Cs and he says
he wants no more of school, but I can't imagine him doing
anything dull or routine. As his friends make plans for college, he's noticeably down, already anticipating feeling like a
"failure" after high school. Do you have any advice for helping a teenager like this plan for his future?*

Dear Concerned Parent:

I've been trying to learn as much as possible about the
lives of successful adults who struggled in school as children and teenagers. I anticipate that Kurt will someday
join the ranks of these individuals, whom by the way we
see as extremely resilient and courageous people. There is
much that we can learn from these individuals, and the lessons they can teach us may someday prove extremely valuable in helping other kids having to contend with similar
adversities.

Many successful adults who struggled in school were,
like Kurt, talented in a variety of areas. Looking back over
their school histories however, their strengths may not
have extended to reading, mathematics, or subjects requir-
ing organizational skills. It probably shouldn't surprise us
that for many of these individuals, their identities formed
around the few things that they struggled most with, as
these areas comprised the vast majority of activities they
were required to do during their years in school. Their
wide-ranging gifts seemed to do little to alter their views of
themselves. Make no mistake — these individuals were very
talented. Some were gifted in their ability to solve prob-

lems in unique and inventive ways. Some were gifted artistically and creatively. And some were extremely talented in the way that they related to people. What they were not gifted in were such things as reading, spelling, multiplying, dividing, remembering where they put things, or doing things that required a lot of repetition. As kids, some of these individuals also found school to be very boring. During their school years, these kids were stimulation seekers, always looking for exciting things to do.

So herein lie a couple of questions that I'm sure greatly concern you, and which, for some time now, have also greatly concerned us: First, how can we help these multi-talented kids start to see themselves more accurately, that is, as individuals with multiple talents who aren't strong within specific academic and/or attention areas? And second, how can we help steer multi-talented young people, who may not be strong within specific academic related areas, into career paths that will provide them the opportunity to showcase and nourish their talents?

Our search for answers to these questions has led us to the growing field of research on human resilience. . . . Let me briefly share with you some of the findings we've come upon that are helping us guide many young people, and which may also be of some help to you.

Successful individuals who overcame earlier childhood adversities began, at some point, to define themselves more around their multiple talents than around their few areas of vulnerability. The fact that they had areas of talent and areas of vulnerability didn't distinguish them from most of us. Actually, when you think about it, what seems to distinguish us most from each other, at least in terms of how we define ourselves, is where our talents lie, and to what degree our talents are nourished and seen as meaningful as we develop.

Many of these individuals had the good fortune of being provided with opportunities to express their talents in meaningful ways and to have their talents recognized and valued by others, particularly others whom they saw as important people in their lives. So talents and abilities need outlets for expression. Ever notice how happy Kurt is after a good acting performance?

Being able to showcase our talents, and to have them valued by important people in our lives, helps us define our identities around that which we do best. This is how people develop a sense of mastery. The reverse is true as well. If you spend a disproportionate amount of your life doing the few things you do poorly, and do these things around important people who see you only in this light, you're apt to define yourself in harsh and devaluing ways.

Many successful adults who didn't do well in school as kids and teenagers also often speak of a very important person in their lives who might have served as a mentor, or who might have been very skilled at something they were skilled at, and who made them aware of career paths they weren't aware of before. Someday, there will be professionals who are trained in identifying and opening up career paths for multi-talented individuals who aren't gifted within specific academic related areas. Many counselors today think of vocational schools as the only career path for kids who didn't do well in school. Now don't misunderstand me. Vocational schools serve an extremely valuable role in training individuals to do valued, needed jobs. The point here is that in the future, as we become more knowledgeable about the many different paths that successful adults took to get where they are, vocational school will serve as one viable option. If your dream can be realized through vocational school, then that may prove to be your path. It also may provide you with an opportunity to learn a skill to support yourself while you pursue another dream that may carry with it greater risks, but which compels you to at least give it your very best try.

Another thing that we're learning about successful adults who struggled in school is that somewhere during their lifespan they found different words, a different language, that helped them legitimize the pain and demoralization they experienced in their earlier school years. They stopped defining themselves the way they used to, which was generally in very negative terms. They came to understand that they tried their best, that there were things that they could and couldn't control, and that they may have actually done pretty well under the circumstances.

Many of these successful adults also cite the presence of a special person in their lives, who served as a buffer or protective influence. Often, but not always, this was a parent. This special individual, time and again, was there to dry the child's tears and encourage him to go on and try his best. The child's frustration and pain, and the special person's frustration and pain, often persisted for years and years. In the long run however, being there time and again counted, more than words could convey; a caring, concerned individual who stood by you unconditionally, and who always thought of you as special. . . .

And finally, a brief message to Kurt. While you may not realize it, you represent a group of individuals who possess a type of resilience that has become the focus of many professional people around the country. These people (of which I am one) feel that individuals like yourself have many lessons to teach. Bear in mind that your friends have no real idea what school has felt like for you. You've been tested in ways that your friends haven't. You've stood strong, despite what likely have been some very stressful times. Individuals like yourself often become stronger as a result of this. It's like you develop "psychological antibodies." Future stresses down the road somehow don't seem so big. This isn't always the case for kids who sailed through school smoothly. Some of these kids have escaped having to contend with significant obstacles in their path. These obstacles will likely appear someday, in one form or another. They too will be tested, like you were. I hope they can stand up as well.

You and your school counselor share something in common. Neither of you know much about the potentially wonderful things that lie in store for you in the future. I hope that you can spend some time getting to know, or perhaps even working around special people who love doing the same things that you love doing. Some of these endeavors sound as though they involve theater and music. Volunteer your time working around these people. Speak to people at your local colleges and universities that teach music and drama, and see if they have any ideas. It's important that you speak with people who feel passionately about the areas of talent that you possess, and who have carved out successful careers for themselves. These people may have ideas that you haven't thought about.

In closing, let me just say, Kurt, that I'm typing this letter a few hours after returning from the movies, where I just saw a movie that was directed by Steven Spielberg. The story told to me about Steven Spielberg was that he didn't do so great in school. His family, however, encouraged his creative and expressive talents. Reportedly, at a relatively early age he was already experimenting with a home movie camera. Talent meeting opportunity. Keep in mind that Steven Spielberg's talents, and those of many other well-known artists, are talents that usually aren't highlighted and nourished in most schools, as we've designed them. Nonetheless, they are extraordinarily talented individuals. In the future, Kurt, when our society becomes more aware of the diversity of human talents, and the need to nourish all of them, there'll be more options for students like yourself. For now, you're going to have to be a bit of a trailblazer. Keep in mind that you're in some great company.

The Search for Meaning

Individuals who experienced and overcame traumatic events in their lives sometimes speak of the valuable lessons they've learned (Janoff-Bulman, 1992). It's as though the traumatic experience taught them something very important, and this valuable knowledge has helped focus them and given them a new purpose in life. This ability to derive important lessons from painful life events represents a significant coping strategy (Janoff-Bulman). In Janoff-Bulman's extensive research with survivors of traumatic life events, she often heard individuals mention how they no longer take life for granted, that life has taken on new meaning. These individuals also speak of a new appreciation of themselves; they recognize a kind of inner strength and resilience that went unrecognized before.

During his time in a concentration camp in Nazi Germany, Victor Frankl (1963) realized that there is always a choice as to how adversities can be viewed. He saw that even the most dire life circumstances can be looked upon in ways that offer individuals special meaning, and that this special meaning can allow one to endure events and experiences that on the surface look impossible to bear. Some individuals who have lived through traumatic life experiences feel that meaning and purpose can be extracted from all life events. There's always a choice, they feel, in how negative life events are ultimately faced and interpreted. Even the most stressful and painful experiences can be faced with dignity and courage. These core beliefs are protective. They can soften the blow of future life stresses.

Researchers are studying and documenting the ways in which individuals ascribe new meaning to difficult life events and how this new meaning helps them endure and overcome challenging life experiences. In one study, researchers interviewed a group of individuals who lived through a major fire and found that more than half of them derived some form of special meaning from the experience (Thompson, 1985). Some felt that they were lucky that more serious consequences didn't occur from the fire; some felt better off than others who lived through the experience; and some said that they were able to think about the positive aspects and not about the negative ones. Thompson found that those individuals who were able to derive some special meaning from the experience coped better than those who could not.

Learning about Others Who Overcame Similar Adversities

Having a chance to learn about others who overcame similar risks and adversities in their earlier years can instill a sense of hope. It is proof that things can change. Resilience through the Life Span is a new project in San Diego that offers this opportunity to children, families, and young adults (see appendix). The project videotapes interviews of people who overcame difficult childhoods—successful adults who were raised under abusive or violent conditions, who grew up in impoverished surroundings, or who had very bad experiences during their school years due perhaps to learning and/or attention difficulties. Four questions are asked during these taped interviews: (1) What have you learned? (2) As you look back, what were some of the strengths that you feel you had, or that you developed, that helped you through the tough times? (3) Were there any turning point experiences that you can remember, which led to things changing for the better? and (4) Based on what you've learned, what would you tell others who are going through what you went through? Participants are allowed to talk for as long as they like.

The purpose of the project is to make these videotapes available to children, families, and young adults who are contending with similar life experiences, but who have lost hope that things can change. These tapes show them that things *can* change; they can hear and see it from those who have overcome similar challenges.

Alan, who is 45 years old and working for a computer firm, had never heard of Tourette's disorder until he was in his thirties. He chose to be interviewed so that others might learn from his experiences. Alan spent many years of his childhood in and out of special schools and mental health centers. No one ever diagnosed him correctly. "In those years," says Alan, "nobody knew much about it. . . . They thought I was psychotic. . . . I sometimes would make these strange noises. . . . I would stop making them for awhile, then I would start again. My parents, my teachers, my doctors, they all thought I was crazy . . . and I thought I was crazy. . . . Nobody knew about Tourette's disorder. . . . What an amazing thing it was to find out one day that there were other people with the same strange symptoms that I struggle with . . . and that we're not crazy . . . that it's actually a neurological problem." Since learning to view the condition he struggled with for so long in a new light, Alan has become very active in a local support group in his community that advocates for the needs of children and adults with Tourette's disorder.

Resources that are Helping Others Find the Words

Several excellent books, videos, and other resource materials are helping children, families, and young adults, as well as educators and health care professionals, see various risks and adverse conditions in a new way. These resources cover both environmental and neurobiological risks.*

Barbara Lewis (1992) wrote a book titled *Kids with Courage*, which tells true stories of resilient youth who have done brave and courageous things, despite having to contend with difficult challenges and crises in their lives. Their stories are intended to help others see that they too can do brave and courageous things, and that their actions may someday help others who face challenges similar to their own.

*See appendix for additional information regarding these and other resources.

A counselor who works with child abuse victims is applying this idea to his work with children and teenagers. He helps child abuse victims tell their stories of courage so others might learn from their experience.

Maria is one his clients. She is 14 years old and a "kid with courage." Until recently, she was being sexually molested by her previous stepfather and was afraid to tell anyone about it. Eventually she told her story to her mother and then to her counselor. The counselor is helping Maria see her willingness to stand up and talk about the ordeal she has lived through as a sign of courage. He is helping her to tell her story in her own words, words that legitimize and validate the pain she has endured. With her counselor's help, she is writing her story so that others can read it. Maria wants to pass on what she is learning to other children and teenagers who are experiencing or have experienced a similar ordeal so that they will know they are not alone and that what is happening to them is not their fault. In fact, she says, each day that they go to school, and try real hard, is a sign of their courage. Maria also hopes that those experiencing what she experienced will be able to come forward and get help.

In the past, there were few resources available to help educators and health care providers recognize the behavioral, emotional, and physiological consequences of exposure to traumatic life events. Fortunately, however, some excellent ones are now available. One such excellent resource is a five-part video series, titled "Understanding Psychological Trauma." The series captures the overwhelming psychological effects of exposure to traumatizing events, both on adults and children. The range of symptoms one can display are also explained, as are the things that traumatized children and adults need in order to begin the healing process.

Several teachers, school counselors, and health care providers have been using the video series as part of their ongoing efforts to better understand the needs of traumatized children and their families. These training materials have provided them with a better appreciation of the effects that overwhelming stress can have upon otherwise healthy children and adults. A new language is provided to explain behavioral and emotional reactions that are sometimes observed among children. Viewers learn about how specific abusive behaviors that a traumatized child witnesses, or is on the receiving end of, can be re-enacted at school or on the playground. The same specific abusive actions that the child witnesses or experiences may be played out by the child on completely innocent children at school. Not knowing how behaviors can be re-enacted by traumatized children will lead many to assume that the child is behaving this way because of oppositional motives or deep-rooted psychological problems. As a result, the interventions we'll choose may be very different from the kinds of intervention the child really needs.

This series of training videos helps educators, health care providers, and other caring individuals who might comprise an individual's circle of support better understand the often confusing reactions that can occur among those confronting traumatic experiences. It shows the behavioral and physiological consequences that can arise from this type of exposure, and it helps us appreciate that these reactions can occur among otherwise healthy individuals.

Books can also help parents, teachers, and counselors teach children with learning disabilities to see their "differences" in a new light. For example, *Different is Not Bad, Different is the World*, by Sally Smith (1994), director of the Lab School in Washington, DC, is written for grades 2–6. The book is about how all people are different and explores the different ways we live and learn. The book can also be used to help children without disabilities to understand that everyone has both strengths and weaknesses and to recognize each other's many talents. *Different is Not Bad, Different is the World* teaches that being different can be a nuisance sometimes, but a child can still go to college, can still grow up to be what he or she wants to be.

Color Me Successful: The Outstanding Learning Disabled Achievers Honored by the Lab School of Washington (Smith, 1993), a coloring book depicting drawings and pictures of famous people with learning disabilities, can be used as a companion to *Different is Not Bad*. The drawings are of famous athletes, movie stars, politicians, and scholars. Multiple areas of talent are honored.

There is an excellect video, "Understanding Learning Disabilities: How Difficult Can This Be," by Richard Lavoie (1989) that has helped many parents appreciate what their son or daughter struggles with. (The video is also known as the F.A.T. City Workshop; F.A.T. stands for frustration, anxiety, and tension.) The video takes educators, health care providers, and parents and siblings of learning disabled children through different simulation exercises that place them in the shoes of the learning disabled child. They get to see and feel what it is like to be confronted with academic tasks that cannot be completed no matter how hard one tries, in a setting where one is being judged based upon his or her ability to succeed.

Learning to Talk about Painful Life Experiences

Marlene didn't learn to talk about her traumatizing childhood experiences until she was 22 years old. Marlene had suffered ongoing physical and sexual abuse by her stepfather, and never revealed this to anyone. She struggled emotionally and behaviorally throughout her childhood and teenage years. She made several suicide attempts and was hospitalized on three different occasions. There were also times when Marlene ran away from home and lived on the streets. Despite seeing a number of counselors, she never told anyone what she was going through at home. And no one asked.

At age 22, she sought help from a therapist experienced in

working with victims of childhood trauma. Marlene finally began to put words to the horrifying experiences that she endured as a child. "It still hurts to think about the past," she says. "I guess the awful memories may never go away. But they don't control me anymore. They don't overwhelm me. I control them."

Researchers have shown that when we talk about traumatic experiences that we have endured, we allow ourselves to rework the experience cognitively (Pennebaker & Blihr-Beall, 1986). We open up greater opportunities for seeing the experience in a different light. If we simply think about painful life events over and over, we are more likely to re-experience the same thoughts over and over. Janoff-Bulman (1992) feels this is one reason why talking about traumatic experiences can be important to the healing process. She reminds us, though, that disclosure sometimes results in greater initial distress. Although it is more distressing initially to talk about the experience than to remain silent, the long-term benefits, far outweigh the short-term distress.

Those who have endured exposure to traumatizing life experiences have to learn to talk about what they have been through (van der Kolk, 1994); they have to learn to put words to their experiences. Yet, abused, neglected, and traumatized children will not usually tell you how they feel. Fortunately, children can find the words to validate painful life experiences in other ways. For example, in teaching children to stop blaming themselves for traumatic events that have occurred in their lives, Beverly James (1989) has the child stand by a window and shout out for the world to hear, "It's not my fault!" The child first tells the universe, says James, and then tells himself. "It's like peeling an orange — one starts from the outside and moves inward" (James, 1989, p. 70). In helping children growing up in inner-city war zones cope with the violence they see, James Garbarino (1993) compiled an activities workbook that encourages children to express their emotions through drawings and stories. The activities teach them about the meaning and effects of violence, and the feelings that children can have when they witness it. Feelings are legitimized and validated. Desensitizing the child to the trauma, helping him to express emotions related to the traumatic experience, and helping him to not see the experience as the central theme in his life are key to the healing process (van der Kolk, 1994).

Learning to See Psychiatric Illness, Alcoholism, and other Disabling Conditions in a New Light

Steven, age 16, and Teddy, age 8, are brothers who share a close personal bond. They both also feel very close to their mother, who has been ill of late. Their mother has a serious depressive disorder, and on a few occasions over the last couple of years has had to be hospitalized for her own safety.

Teddy thought that his mother became ill because of him, because he sometimes didn't clean his room and finish all his homework. This bothered him a great deal, but he never told anyone about how he was feeling. Behavior problems were increasing both at school and at home, but no one connected these with something that might be troubling Teddy — nobody, that is, except Steven, who knew his brother well and knew something was wrong.

Steven spent a lot of time with Teddy, and they talked quite a bit. Teddy learned that his mother had been ill for a long time, long before he was even born. He learned that not only didn't he cause his mother's problems, but also that his mother loved him very much and that she feels he's a wonderful son. Teddy also learned that when Steven was his age, he felt the very same way.

In time, Teddy's behavior problems disappeared. He also started helping out more around the house. Steven kept a watchful eye on him, looking out for any signs that he might be feeling troubled again, but these troubled feelings didn't return.

Many resilient children being raised by seriously ill parents often learned early on that the illness they saw existed not within themselves, but within the parent. As a result, they were less likely to feel personally responsible for certain unusual or harsh reactions they encountered at home, to attribute these reactions to something they did, and to believe that these reactions are in some way their fault. They were able to see that these confusing and hard-to-comprehend behaviors were not a reflection of how their parent felt about them. They began to see their adversity differently, which in turn served to reduce any long-term damaging effects.

Wolin and Wolin (1993) studied the lives of adult children of alcoholic parents, including how they were adapting as adults and the quality of their relationships. Contrary to the popular perception, they discovered that children of alcoholics do not necessarily develop serious drinking problems. Wolin and Wolin's study revealed that many adult children of alcoholic parents currently lead productive lives. They feel this is an area that warrants more of our attention, and that there are lessons to be learned from these survivors.

According to Wolin and Wolin, at some point during their lives, these adult survivors learned to see themselves as strong and courageous, and not as damaged. They learned to see earlier childhood adversities in a new light. There's something wrong here, they realized, and it's not me. This capacity for insight served an important protective function. "While you cannot change the past, you can change the way you understand it. . . . You can frame your story around themes of your resilience or themes of your damage. You can find reasons to be proud in some of your worst memories, or you can let yourself be overwhelmed by the harm of it all" (Wolin & Wolin, 1993, p. 207).

This reframing process can be learned by anyone who has endured or is currently enduring the effects of growing up in a home with an alcoholic parent. "Anybody can be a reframer.

It's not something that only happens in therapy" (Wolin &
Wolin, 1994). An important part of this reframing process is
accepting that one is not a helpless victim of circumstances.
"The promise of sympathy that comes with a victim's status is
enticing bait. But if you take it, you will be helplessly hooked
to your pain" (Wolin & Wolin, 1993, p. 7).

Jerry is 35 years old, happily married with 2 children, and
enjoys a successful law practice. He recalls a very unhappy
childhood, however, the result of a stepfather who was an
alcoholic and who became physically violent when he drank.
Jerry remembers the feelings of terror that overcame him when
his stepfather came home drunk, and he remembers the times
that his stepfather beat him, for reasons he could never understand. Jerry also remembers the way he used to blame himself
for his family's difficulties and the rage he felt inside toward
his stepfather. He harbored these feelings until he was 20 years
old, and never revealed them to anyone. Then he began seeing
a counselor at college who knew a great deal about alcoholism
and how it affects families. For the first time Jerry began hearing about how many other children of alcoholics grow up feeling the way he did, and he began appreciating how strong and
courageous he had actually been all those years to be able to
endure the beatings. While painful memories didn't disappear,
Jerry learned to view earlier events in his life differently. He
has grown to recognize how resilient he had actually been as a
child. He has also come to recognize and appreciate similar
characteristics in many of the individuals he comes in contact
with through his law practice; individuals who also endured
hurtful childhood experiences.

A Closer Look at the Reframing Process

In their study of highly successful learning disabled adults,
Gerber et al. (1990) noted how important it was for these indi-

viduals to recognize and accept the presence of their disability. They also showed that the degree of acceptance varies significantly. I know of two learning disabled individuals that have recognized and accepted their disability, yet one spends large amounts of energy covering it up, while the other engages in constructive actions that significantly minimize any negative effects from the disability. The reframing process can occur in varying degrees, and the degree to which it occurs can have major implications on the level of success one achieves.

Gerber et al. (1990) note four stages in the reframing process: recognition, acceptance, understanding, and action. Each stage relates and interacts closely with the others. According to the authors, some highly successful learning disabled individuals seemed capable of moving through all stages almost simultaneously, while others seemed to move through them in a sequential or step-by-step fashion. And some individuals did it early in their lives, some later.

1. The recognition stage occurs when one realizes that he does things differently, because he has a disability. The authors quoted one highly successful learning disabled adult: "You need to find out who you are and you are not going to succeed out there if you can't look at yourself in the mirror. If you can't deal with who you are and recognize your gifts and your disadvantages, you are not going to make it."

2. During the acceptance stage, the individual learns to accept the disability as real. It doesn't define him, though; he recognizes his strengths and talents and moves ahead. But he also knows that he has a disability, and that he will have to do some things differently, things that others without a disability might not have to do. The authors quoted a highly successful learning disabled professor: "I need to be proud of myself. As long as I was ashamed of being learning disabled, it was difficult to succeed. It's

only been since the acknowledgment and use of appropriate services (that success came)."

3. The need for understanding represents the third stage in
the reframing process. An individual has to understand
his strengths as well as his weaknesses. Once this understanding is reached, he has to build on those strengths
and find ways to work around and compensate for the
weaknesses. A very successful lawyer was quoted as saying: "The biggest advantage is that once you realize you
can't do all these things, you become good at finding
alternative solutions and at making the most of what you
have. . . . I think the anger, sense of injustice, and wisdom which that situation has given me has helped me."

4. The final stage is the action stage. The individual has to
take action.Recognizing, accepting, and understanding
his disability is not enough; he has to do things in new,
different, and creative ways in order to reach his goals.

Reframing one's own disability is not easy. Gerber et al.
(1990) cite examples of highly successful learning disabled
adults who, at earlier times in their lives, were terror-struck at
the thought of other people finding out about some of the
things they couldn't do. Yet reframing can and does occur.
And it occurs at a much more complete level among learning
disabled individuals who have achieved a high level of vocational success. Educators and health care providers can help
individuals in this reframing process. As already mentioned,
there are excellent resource and training materials available.
The stigma is also waning, thanks to many highly successful
people who are coming forward to talk about their disabilities,
including movie stars, CEOs, lawyers, doctors, professors, and
others. Persons with learning disabilities can now see they are
in good company and that they no longer have to feel shame
or embarrassment.

Over the years, Adam Kline (1993) has come to understand

his learning disabilities in a new light. Not only has he been able to reframe how he views his own learning differences, he has also grown keenly aware of how others who learn differently feel and how they have suffered. Adam is in the action phase of the reframing process. He is extremely outspoken about the needs of children and adults with learning disabilities, and conducts workshops around the country to help others become more aware of those needs. Some people who have heard him speak think that he comes off angry and sounds a bit melodramatic sometimes. Adam says, "I'm not angry. I'm enraged. I see things happening to children today that happened to me in the 1960s. Melodramatic? I'm not dramatic enough. These are kids in pain. And we're treating them the same way I was treated" (Kline, 1993). Speaking from experience, Adam stresses how important it is for children with learning disabilities to understand why it is that they learn differently. Knowing something is wrong and not knowing what it is can be paralyzing. You need to know what it is that makes it so hard for you to learn, says Adam, and then you need to learn how to be your own best advocate.

Reframing one's own disability is especially difficult for children. After helping a child understand the nature of learning disabilities, one cruel remark from someone at school may send the child back to square one. But this reframing process definitely can be accomplished, and its importance is becoming increasingly clear. It was central in the lives of highly successful learning disabled adults, and it will likely be central to anyone, child or adult, wishing to establish a similarly positive life trajectory.

"A Little Piece of Mind"

Jerry Mills, who is both a school teacher and a songwriter, struggled his entire life with attention deficit disorder, and never realized what his problem was. That is, not until Michael, a student in his class, was diagnosed with ADD. Jerry recognized that he was much like Michael when he was his age. He decided to go for an evaluation, and soon learned that he too had ADD. After being diagnosed and receiving some help, Jerry wrote this song titled "A Little Piece of Mind" (Mills, 1993):

How can simple words explain
The ceaseless thoughts, the endless pain
The doubts that you were sometimes sane, while never bein' sure?
Your thoughts were racin' round and round,
Feet were rarely on the ground
Your mind a spring that was overwound
Yar whole darn life a blur.
And though no one ever understood you
How could they when not even you could?
You couldn't slow down, though you wished you would
So you could just unwind.
But a million thoughts would fill your head
And distract you from the life you led
When in fact you'd always wished instead
That one day you could find . . .
A little piece of mind . . .

As a kid you went to school but you couldn't sit still
Soon the teacher had had her fill
So she used her whip to crack your will,
And at six years old you cried.
But with each new year what would it bring?
Usually the same old thing
Like a puppet tangled in its strings
You get all tied up inside.

Because while you were always geared to go
The word you always heard was "No"

And so you even came to doubt, the things
That you might think about.
You'd see yourself as out of place, a loser in the human race
Until you even lost all hope that you would ever learn to cope.
You couldn't seem to keep your cool
You'd cry inside while playin' the fool.
You'd walk alone, behind, ahead
And soon regret hard words you said
And as the days and weeks and years
Fueled frustrations, fostered fears,
Deep within your dark despair
The will to persevere was there . . .

So you learned to count the ceiling holes,
Race along with restless souls
While some set sights on dreams and goals, you were runnin' blind.
Until you met a boy who happened to be diagnosed with ADD.
And thanks to Michael now you see

That finally you can find a little piece of mind . . .
Finally I'm learning to find . . . a little piece of mind.

Conclusion

Vera Fahlberg (1995) recalls working with an extremely resilient child many years ago. The child was sexually abused by her mother, who later abandoned her. The girl was subsequently placed in a foster home, where she adjusted remarkably well. Her foster mother described her as happy and healthy. Fahlberg, who came to know this girl, concurred. The girl seemed happy and healthy; but she wasn't supposed to be. Not only was she sexually abused, she was also abandoned by her mother.

When Fahlberg asked the child how she felt about her

mother leaving her, she replied, "Imagine a mother doing that to a child. She must be really sick." The girl said that her mother had warned her that one day she wouldn't be there for her; one day she would leave and someone from the welfare department would come and get her. Sure enough, one day the girl's mother left. The girl then went outside and waited for the person from the welfare department to come pick her up. In a very odd sort of way, the girl's mother prepared her for things to come.

For this child, protection originated from within. She was extraordinarily resilient. She was a healthy child being raised in a very disturbed environment, and somehow she figured this out. At a young age she was able to see the adversities that she faced in a different light, and was able to find the words to legitimize and validate the pain she was having to endure. Hope was never lost. This little girl "beat the odds."

But in cases like this, there is usually more protection coming from somewhere to buffer the child from exposure to harsh realities that can be expected to wear anyone down, regardless of their resilience. Something is changing the odds. Often it is a combination of things. In the chapter that follows, I'll discuss how individuals, schools, afterschool programs, and different services are helping to shield children from the damaging effects of risks that will likely persist in their lives for many years, and how, in the process, they're changing the odds.

Chapter 6

Buffers: Reducing Exposure to Adverse Conditions

Environmental disadvantages and advantages tend to persist. There is continuity in both advantage and disadvantage (Rutter & Rutter, 1993). If you are confronting adversities in one environment, it is very likely that you are also confronting adversities in other environments. The child growing up in impoverished surroundings will likely attend a school where the incidence of violence and crime is very high. A child growing up in an affluent home will likely attend a very good school.

Children confronting multiple adversities also stand a pretty good chance of having to confront the same multiple adversities years later. If children are born into poverty, they will likely be raised in poverty. They will be poor as infants, poor when they begin school, and poor when they become teenagers. If children are born into a violent household, they will likely be raised in a violent household. Children confronting multiple adversities who show problems early in their lives may continue to show problems years later because the adversities they have to contend with persist.

Many researchers now believe that if these adversities are removed, if later experiences in a child's life are good ones, then adverse or depriving experiences early in a child's life may not permanently alter development (Rutter & Rutter, 1993). Given that children are usually unable to alter the adverse conditions that confront them, no matter how hard they try, and given that these adverse conditions may be around for a long time, it's imperative that we provide buffers to shield these children as best we can.

The School as a Protective Influence

Parents and health care professionals have perhaps no greater resource than the neighborhood school for protecting, nourishing, and stimulating children raised under conditions of severe adversity (Garmezy, 1991; Rutter, 1979a). Schools serve all children, regardless of their disadvantages in other life areas. They can stimulate and nourish talents which might otherwise go unnoticed; remediate specific areas of vulnerability; enhance social and interpersonal abilities necessary for friendships and other relationships to develop; permanently alter the developmental trajectories of children who would otherwise develop serious emotional and behavioral difficulties; and they can instill a sense of hope and future in children and families who would otherwise give up. Positive school experiences can also neutralize painful events occurring in other life areas. In her study of abused children who were adapting well as adults,

Zimrin (1986) found this to be the case for a number of children.

Research has also shown that two schools in the same poor neighborhood can have entirely different effects on children's lives, depending upon the resources and quality of the school. Rutter (1979a) studied two different schools in the same economically disadvantaged area and found very different rates of behavioral difficulties, truancy, academic problems, and delinquency. For example, one had a rate of delinquency that was three times higher than the other. A closer examination of the two schools revealed that the school with the lower delinquency rate demonstrated, among other characteristics, more effective classroom management strategies and a greater degree of classroom structure. Also, the attitudes and beliefs among the administrative and teaching staff at this school fostered the acquisition of important social and cognitive skills among the students. The point here is that the students attending the two different schools were all exposed to the same environmental risks. The schools were different, not the children attending them. One school offered greater protection than the other.

Marguerite is a single working African American mother who just moved into a new neighborhood, and had to decide which of two different elementary schools would best meet the educational and emotional needs of her two children. Her two children had been through a lot over the last few years: Their grandmother, who helped raise them, died suddenly; their father, whom they were also very close to, remarried and moved to another city; and, they had not been progressing well at their previous school and the school counselor didn't know why. Both children were said to be at risk of being retained. Marguerite was becoming increasingly worried about her children and about how best to meet their educational and emotional needs.

A few words about the two schools she had to choose from.

The streets surrounding each of the schools were considered very dangerous. One didn't walk the streets alone at night, and most people didn't walk them alone during the daytime either. Drugs were everywhere you looked and children and teenagers had ready access to them. The crime rate in each neighborhood was among the highest in the city. The neighborhoods surrounding each school were very much alike. The two schools that Marguerite had to choose from, however, were different. One school, and the one that Marguerite ultimately chose to enroll her children in, was based upon the Comer process. Marguerite made the right choice.

The Comer Process

My first encounter with a school that embraced the Comer process occurred several years ago, when a family invited me to a school meeting with their 11-year-old son's teacher. Their son was struggling academically and emotionally, and the parents and the teacher didn't know why. They all wanted to meet in order to explore possible causes of the child's difficulties. I remember walking into the meeting room, expecting to see three people—one teacher and the child's mother and father; instead, I saw 10 more—the principal, resource specialist, school counselor, school nurse, school psychologist, and several aides and community volunteers were also there. They were all there to talk about how they might be able to help one 11-year-old child and support a set of very worried parents. If you think all schools are alike, if you think it is not possible to mobilize community resources to support local schools, if you think it is not possible to address children's individual learning needs, or if you are feeling kind of hopeless about the educational system in general, visit a school that embraces the Comer process.

James Comer, professor of Psychiatry at the Yale University Child Study Center, developed a model school program that has, among its core features, a mechanism for involving parents in all aspects of decision making when it comes to educating their children and a mechanism for dealing with wide-ranging developmental needs, including a child's emotional needs. School team members are trained to deal with emerging mental health needs of children if and when they occur, through an array of services that can be tailored to each child and family's unique life circumstances. Community resources, volunteers, paraprofessionals, teachers, administrators, school mental health resources, and family members all work together to create a community school designed to meet students' educational and emotional needs. Parents are full partners in the process, and are involved in all levels of decision making.

School as a Buffer for the Child with ADHD

The child with ADHD usually knows the rules for doing what he's supposed to do, and has the skills to do it. "ADHD is not a problem of knowing what to do, it's a problem of doing what we know. It's a problem of performance. Arrange the environment properly, and the skill will be shown" (Barkley, 1994).

Jeff is 8 years old and a third-grader attending a small private school in southern California. His teachers say that he's doing just great, and Jeff agrees. This is quite a turnaround. Last year, in the second grade, Jeff attended a different school and was failing. He dreaded going to school each morning, and on some mornings actually became physically ill. Jeff had been diagnosed as having an attention problem and writing difficulties, and was receiving extra help from the school staff, who were extremely caring and very motivated to help Jeff in any way that they could. Even so, his grades didn't improve. Then his mother switched him to a small private school she had heard about from some friends. The classes are much smaller in size, allowing teachers to give each student much more individualized attention. Jeff likes his new school and says that he's learning a lot. His writing skills haven't improved much, but his teachers allow him to communicate his ideas verbally, which has been a great help. He is also learning how to use a computer, which he really enjoys working on. His parents and teachers feel that he'll be able to do much better on writing assignments in the future as he becomes more proficient in his keyboarding skills. As Russell Barkley (1994) said, "Arrange the environment properly, and the skill will be shown." This school provides an excellent illustration of this idea, and has come to represent an important protective influence in Jeff's life.

After the School Day Ends: Neighborhood Organizations that Buffer and Protect

32-year-old Antonio graduated from college with a bachelor of arts in education and currently teaches full time at the same inner-city high school that he attended as a teenager. Antonio's life is going well, and he enjoys teaching. As a teenager however, he struggled up until his junior year in high school. He followed the wrong crowd, and for a time he and his friends were experimenting with drugs. At one point he was thinking about dropping out of school. It was around the time that his parents divorced and his father moved away. There were two things that Antonio says kept him from completely ruining his life: basketball and his basketball coach.

During his junior and senior years of high school, Antonio was on the school basketball team. He loved basketball, and looking back it's clear that the basketball coach loved Antonio. The coach kept a very watchful eye on him during those last two years. At the direction of his coach, Antonio practiced almost every afternoon for hours, sometimes in the school gym and sometimes at the local YMCA. By the time he got home for dinner, he was exhausted. Whatever time he had left in the evening was used for studying. If he failed any more subjects he would be off the team so Antonio's coach arranged for a tutor to help him with subjects that were especially hard for him.

During those last two years of high school, Antonio didn't spend much time around the friends he had previously done drugs with. He didn't have the time. He was too busy and too tired.

The coach's formula for keeping Antonio away from drugs was simple: Give Antonio something to do that he loves doing, have him do it from the time right after school ends until it's time for dinner, and make sure he does it in places where people do not do drugs. The coach knew how imperative it was for some children and teenagers to have access to structured and supervised activities after school, and he was a master at structuring them.

While afterschool programs and neighborhood organizations can serve as important resources in the lives of all children and teenagers, they may serve as especially important buffers in the lives of inner city children growing up in our poorest and most violent communities. McLaughlin, Irby, and Langman (1994) studied how some afterschool programs are able to be this kind of buffer; how they're able to shield children and teenagers from some of the risks that surround them. They refer to these programs as "urban sanctuaries." It has been estimated that 40% of the waking hours of teenagers is uncommitted time (Carnegie Council on Adolescent Development, 1994). For a child growing up in an inner city, the time between the end of school and the time that he falls asleep may represent the most dangerous portion of the day.

Of the thousands of inner-city programs designed to serve children, which are the most protective? Which are the ones that children choose to join, and then stay with for a long time? And why do these programs work so well, while other equally well-intentioned programs, with equally trained and committed staff, don't? Mclaughlin et al. (1994) spent time with teenagers and youth advocates in more than 60 organizations in three large metropolitan areas to find the answers to these questions.

Lessons Learned from the Study of Urban Sanctuaries

Inner-city teenagers often stayed away from programs that presented a negative view of inner-city youth. Prevention and remediation programs were often seen as demeaning and punitive (McLaughlin et al., 1994). How organizations referred to themselves also mattered; "afterschool" programs often weren't seen in a positive way because a number of the teenagers had a negative view of school. Some of these teenagers also saw programs that had the best of intentions as totally irrelevant to their needs. They were not offering the kinds of opportunities and activities that mattered most to them. In addition, the successful inner-city programs did not tie themselves to a social problem.

According to the authors, the teenagers who benefited the most from these urban sanctuaries weren't very different from other children and teenagers in their neighborhood. They weren't more gifted or more resilient. They were exposed to the same dangers, the same crime-ridden streets, the same level of poverty, the same level of violence. They *did* differ in the way they attached to an inner-city organization. The organization and the people who ran it provided them with a new way of seeing their future. They had fun, made friends, learned new skills, and felt hopeful.

Common Features of Urban Sanctuaries

McLaughlin et al. (1994) highlighted six urban sanctuaries that they found to be effective programs, that seemed to serve as important buffers in the lives of inner-city youth: the Reggie Jones Gymnasts, Luanna Williams and the Arroyo Girl Scout Troop, Roberto Colon and the Porter Crossing YMCA Gang

Alternatives and Intervention Program (GAIN), Steve Patterson and Cooper House, John Pena and TeenTalk, and Michael Carroll and Building Educational Strategies For Teens (BEST). While these programs are very different from one another, they share some important features:

- They offer safety. Tito, a gang member who participated in one of the programs, was quoted as saying, "Kids can walk around trouble if there is some place to walk to, and someone to walk with" (McLaughlin et al., p. 219).
- The teenagers feel listened to. The program's direction fills some real needs.
- These programs offer opportunities. They teach real skills that can be used years down the road.
- The programs provide exposure to a world outside of the neighborhood.
- The responsibilities that teenagers are required to maintain are real and valued; there are real demands with real deadlines.
- The program rules are clear and there is consistent discipline.
- The programs focus on the future and the role that education can play in this regard. Education is valued and seen as a means to a positive future.

While the individuals who run the successful urban sanctuaries are also very different from one another, they too share some very similar and important qualities:

- They see potential, not pathology. They believe in the youth they work with and see their potential.
- They view these teenagers as largely ignored and poorly served. They are not trying to remediate or fix them, but rather are trying to guide them through the indifference and shield them from the violence.
- These individuals are strongly focused on the positive; they focus on raising expectations and providing a setting

where one could change attitudes and develop skills necessary for a better life.

- These program leaders designed their programs around the needs of the teenagers. This is very different than focusing primarily on the needs of a program. McLaughlin et al. note how easy it is to miss the real needs. Having a trusted adult that's available on a regular basis, at times that can be counted on, may be critical for a teenager who has no reliable adult in his or her life. If a program's main concern is its content (e.g., what curriculum to use for the afternoon education center), it's easy to miss the vital, yet unspoken, needs.
- They believe that they are making a difference in the lives of the teenagers they are serving.
- They desire to give to others what has been given to them — the desire to pass opportunities along.
- These individuals are authentic. Their programs are an expression of their personal talents. Children and teenagers seem to be particularly drawn to programs and program leaders who express and highlight interests and talents that closely match their own.

Returning Home at the End of the Day

We live at a time when some schools use metal detectors to insure that students are not bringing weapons to class. Some schools are very dangerous. Yet, those same schools may be the safest place in the neighborhood. The school may be a safer place than the neighborhood recreation center, which in turn may be a safer place than the housing unit that a child or teenager lives in.

If schools and afterschool programs can serve as buffers, then so can housing units or apartment complexes. Some are able to offer greater protection than others for children and teenagers exposed to multiple sources of danger. For example, Garmezy (1992), described a study of families living in two public housing projects in a very poor neighborhood within a city. The projects were located near one another and comprised of families sharing similar economic, ethnic, racial, and cultural backgrounds, but they produced significantly different outcomes among the resident children: school dropout rate, 7.2% versus 33%; below grade level in reading, 32% versus 70%; crime reports, 46% versus 85%. While even the lower rates of difficulty are terribly unacceptable, the point is that the conditions that children and families were living under made a very significant difference in their day-to-day adaptation and resulted in very different child outcomes.

Mentoring Relationships

You ask me can I do it,
Well don't you understand.
You're the one to answer,
Because I can if you think I can.
I have the courage and the skill,
But these alone won't do.
I must be sure that you believe I can
do what you ask me to.
So whether or not I reach my goals,
In your hand I place the key.
Before I can ever reach heights,
I must know you believe in me.

I Can If You Think I Can
Ivan Fitzwater

A mentor is an individual who forms a meaningful and nurturing bond with another, usually younger, individual. Through this bond, the mentor is able to transfer valuable knowledge, wisdom, and lessons of life that leave a lasting imprint. The relationship is often a powerful force in helping the younger person make the transition into adulthood. The relationship touches the mentor as well, in an emotional way.

Recall Antonio, from our discussion on neighborhood organizations. Looking back on his last two years of high school, Antonio says that his basketball coach was both a coach and a mentor. He learned a lot about life from him, and remembers well some of the long conversations they had after games and practices.

Antonio also talks about one of his students, a junior in high school who is very talented and sensitive, but who suddenly began failing in several classes. He has the skills to make it through college and beyond, but he just stopped trying. Antonio began spending time with this student after school, tutoring him, talking with him, and letting him know how talented he is. As a result of this mentoring relationship, the student has turned things around. He's doing well now. Antonio knew that he could help this teenager: "Something about him reminds me of how I was when I was his age."

Marc Freedman (1993) is studying mentoring programs around the United States. He offers important lessons to individuals wanting to either start or become involved in a mentoring program. Freedman indicates that these lessons are not all positive, but he feels that we have to learn both the positive and nonpositive lessons if future mentoring efforts are to reach their potential. Some of his findings and observations include the following:

1. For children confronting multiple adversities, involvement has to begin early and last for a long time. Some programs start with children when they are in the second grade, and stay in place for six years.
2. In some programs, teenagers who have established men-

toring relationships with adults serve as mentors to younger children. These programs are referred to as "tripartite" programs. Teenagers enjoying mentoring relationships with adults learn to pass the benefits they are deriving on to younger children in need.

3. Having a task to work on together is often important in helping the initial bond to form. Freedman refers to this as "setting up tasks as scaffolding." Tasks can vary. Sometimes they involve actual job functions, where children learn skills that are important in work settings. Sometimes they are educational-based, where certain learning skills are enhanced in the process. And in some mentoring programs, the task involves working together on a community project, where the entire neighborhood benefits in some meaningful way.

4. Most people relate positively to the idea of mentoring relationships. They are simple to understand, direct, one on one, and valued by our culture. But mentoring relationships don't always take hold, despite the best of intentions. Those trying to establish mentoring relationships may also find themselves tested over and over again. Can they endure? Many drop out. For some children, this confirms their view of adults as untrustworthy.

5. Mentors can begin to feel isolated. They need support. In response to this need, some organizations have started self-help support groups for mentors.

The adversities that many children confront growing up in inner cities may persist for years. Freedman points out that there have been no short-term answers that have produced long-term changes. The great excitement we feel about mentoring relationships and our desire to establish programs that support them should take this into account. We are dealing with long-term needs that appear to defy short-term solutions. Mentors won't rebuild decaying neighborhoods or end poverty, they won't enrich schools, and they won't eliminate violence or drug abuse.

The Protective Influence of One Special Person

A little girl was late getting home from school and her mother began to scold her, but then stopped and asked, "Why are you so late?"

"I had to help another girl. She was in trouble," explained the daughter.

"What did you do?"

"Oh, I sat down and helped her cry."

From *Kids' Random Acts of Kindness*.

As I have discussed, many who have endured major hardships in their lives often speak of a special person who was always there to help, when needed the most. He or she offered support, companionship, and guidance. Most of all, he or she really cared. There was no doubting this. Cohen and Wills (1985) have studied the ways in which one valued and supportive relationship can ease the effects of serious life stresses, and refer to this phenomenon as the "buffering hypothesis."

There can be one valued person or several. Close-knit families that love and protect each other provide a network of meaningful relationships. But for those who don't have access to a loving, protective family, that one important relationship can still provide the safety, protection, and support to get them through major life challenges, even those that persist.

Sometimes this person is someone outside of the immediate family. Werner and Smith (1992) found that resilient children growing up in homes where their parents experienced chronic psychiatric problems often were able to detach themselves from the discord at home by spending time with caring adults outside of the immediate family. In one study of teenagers who were able to successfully cope with a parent's affective illness, the teenagers benefited a great deal from the close relationships that they formed not only with other family members, but with friends as well (Beardslee & Podorefsky, 1988). And sometimes the special person is a teacher or a coach; someone who offers support and encouragement at school or during afterschool activities. This person need not serve a mentoring role; he or she can still provide a protective and valued relationship that is emotionally critical to a child's well-being. Zimrin (1986) found this to be the case in her study of individuals who successfully overcame abusive childhood experiences. Most of these individuals mentioned a supportive adult whom they had access to, such as a teacher at school or another person who inspired confidence in them, and encouraged them.

Joey, a 6 year-old foster child, was scared about living in his new foster home. His foster brother, Bobby, who was 9, knew it. They shared a bedroom together, and each night Joey would wake crying from terrible nightmares. Each time Bobby heard Joey crying in the middle of the night, he would get out of his bed, walk over to Joey's bed, and hold him. He would tell Joey not to worry. Bobby's act of compassion was also showing Joey that he wasn't all alone. Joey, feeling comforted and less frightened, would fall back to sleep.

Anthony's teacher knew how difficult it was for Anthony to read and write, and thanks to her efforts at educating some of her other students, so did several of Anthony's classmates. The teacher came up with a way to help Anthony when he felt overwhelmed: As soon as the child sitting next to Anthony noticed him getting tense, he placed his hand gently on Anthony's shoulder. This simple gesture said, "We know it's hard, but it's going to be okay." Anthony could then get up if he'd like, and go sharpen his pencil, or just stretch and take a little break.

He then would have to get back to work. Anthony realized that he had to work much harder than his classmates in order to learn certain things. What he needed, though, was understanding and compassion. His teacher and classmates provided him with this, and he was a much happier child as a result.

Conclusion

Exposure to multiple risks can damage anyone. The more risks we are exposed to, the greater the likelihood that we will be harmed in some way. We may vary in how well we bear up under adversity, but we all seem to have a breaking point. Strength in the face of adversity isn't always enough. Someone may have to offer a helping hand. Someone may have to help buffer us from the emotional impact of the adversities that we're facing. Our struggle to beat the odds can win out if someone or something changes the odds.

In the next chapter, we'll explore another important protective influence that helps neutralize the effects of multiple risk exposure, that can help change the odds.

Chapter 7

Safety Nets: Preventing Negative Chain Reactions

Sometimes, we just can't stop things from spiraling out of control. And those exposed to multiple risks or having to endure the effects of traumatic life experiences are much more likely to have things spiral out of control than others. Children and families caught in this downward spiral need some type of safety net to break their fall; a safety net that allows them to regain a sense of control and stability in their lives. Experiences that short-circuit this negative chain reaction of events, that break the fall so that no further harm occurs, represent another important protective influence.

Creating Safety Nets for One Another

If we're lucky, we have loved ones who come to our aid in times of need — and we in turn will be there should they need us. The fortunate have a circle of support to count on, a safety net to catch them should the pressures overwhelm them to the point that their lives begin to tumble out of control.

There are also some who have this circle of support available, but may not realize it. Ben is a good example. His business was failing, his bills were mounting, he didn't have the money for next month's mortgage payment, and his wife had just been diagnosed with a serious illness. Ben contemplated killing himself.

It was at that time that a friend stepped in to help. Though Ben never confided to his friend how despondent he was, his friend sensed his despair nonetheless. "I couldn't handle all these things if they happened to me," his friend thought. "Ben can't either. He needs some help." The friend called other friends, and together they created a safely net for Ben and his family. They watched Ben's children while he accompanied his wife to her many doctor appointments; they prepared special meals for the family and visited their home almost daily; and they helped to pay some of the family's bills. One day Ben was feeling all alone in the world, with no hope of things improving in his life; the next day the world looked entirely different. "There are problems, sure," said Ben. "But they're solvable. I'll get by. I'm not alone." We never know when circumstances will so overwhelm us that our ability to handle even the smallest of responsibilities will be too difficult. Should such circumstances occur, however, the presence of a safety net in our lives, comprised of a caring circle of support, will prove to be a valuable protective influence.

Paula Lowe (1993) coined the term "carepooling," the act of exchanging help. It's getting help to care for the needs of those you love, whether the loved one is a child, an aging parent, a troubled neighbor, or an ill friend. It's people helping people to take care of each other and those that mean the most to them. Lowe's book, *Carepooling: How to Get the Help You Need to Care For the Ones You Love* (1993) is based on the insights and comments she collected from over 200 caregivers across the United States. She condensed these insights and comments down to practical strategies that people can use to help one another when they share common needs and problems; for example, how to arrange for afterschool child care, how to watch each other's children if there's an emergency, how to work together to keep neighborhoods safe, and how to help care for aging and lonely parents.

During a recent parent support group for parents of children with learning disabilities and attention problems, two families came up with an idea that demonstrates carepooling. Each family had a 7-year-old child with learning disabilities. The two children were also in the same class at school. Both were struggling and both families were worried. The classroom teacher was having a hard time meeting the needs of the two children; it was hard for her to give them the individual attention that she felt they needed. So the two sets of parents and the teacher got together and arranged for a tutor who was knowledgeable about learning disabilities to come to the classroom and work with the two children individually three mornings a week. They also arranged for the tutor to come to each child's home twice a week to provide afterschool tutoring. The plan they put together addressed each child's individual needs and created a very close working relationship between the teacher and the parents. The tutor also helps out in class on the days that she's there, providing a little extra one-on-one attention to some of the other children. This helps to avoid stigmatizing the two children. The program has been very successful. The two families pay for the tutor, but voice no complaints; they feel it's worth the cost, and they especially like having someone available to them who can let them know each week how their children are doing in class. A third family, who also has a child in the class, may join in the tutoring arrangement. Their child doesn't have a learning disability, but they feel his reading skills are a little low, and that he could benefit from some extra help. When the third family joins the pool, the tutoring fees will be split three ways, and the cost will be less for each family.

When a friend of one of the families heard about this program, he was critical. "The school should be paying for those services," he said, "not you. It's their responsibility." The families know this. The year before, and up through the middle of this year, their children were seen by one of the school's resource teachers who is very knowledgeable about learning disabilities. The families hold this teacher in very high regard, but feel that the current plan that they have in place is working better. The resource teacher, in fact, is involved in the plan and consults regularly with the tutor in the classroom.

John and Mary and their teenage daughter, Sarah, are also familiar with carepooling, as is their next door neighbor's 21-year-old daughter, Barbara, a junior in college. John and Mary had been growing increasingly worried about Sarah, who was missing school, voicing extremely critical views of herself, and appearing increasingly withdrawn, sullen, and depressed. She refused to talk to her parents about what might be bothering her or to see a counselor, either individually or with her family. John and Mary shared their worries with Barbara, whom Sarah looked up to, confided in, and trusted. Barbara had also been very concerned about Sarah and volunteered to help out. She offered to take Sarah to some of her college classes and to her part-time job at a local music store. The idea was to keep Sarah busy doing things she enjoyed doing while providing opportunities to share her feelings with an admired friend and confidant. John and Mary were grateful. Sarah especially liked going to work with her older friend and helping her out at the music store. She decided to apply for her own part-time job at a clothing store a few doors down. She got the job and loves it. The difficult period she was going through seems to have passed. She is also doing better in school, feeling better emotionally, and sounding more confident in herself. "Social support doesn't fall from the sky. It can't be bought like a dozen roses. Your employee assistance program or care referral agency does not have a list of helpful friends. . . . Real social support comes from people who know you and help you" (Lowe, 1993, p. 10).

Safety Nets in the Lives of Children in Out-of-Home Placements

Those working in social service and protective service settings are usually all too familiar with the negative chain reaction of events that can occur in the lives of children who are removed for their own safety and protection from extremely abusive and neglectful conditions in their homes. These children sometimes find themselves going to a succession of foster placements. On occasion, one or more of these placements may not have turned out to be a very warm and nurturing home to live in. In some instances, they weren't very safe places either. These are children who were removed from their original homes, a potentially traumatic experience itself, then found themselves exposed to a chain reaction of new, extremely stressful experiences. Professionals who have day-to-day contact with children in foster care feel that the psychological effects of multiple placements on already abused children may be more harmful emotionally than the events that originally required them to be removed from their homes. These children are at risk of having their lives spiral out of control. They need a safety net to break the cycle of negative events occurring in their lives.

The Casey Family Program

One such safety net is the Casey Family Program, with 18 divisions in cities throughout the United States. The program is dedicated to providing a nurturing, stable, and secure foster family for the child who will never be able to live with his birth parents. The foster family will look after the child's needs until he or she is grown and independent. In increasing numbers the Casey Family Program is also extending their safety net to include a child's extended family members, such as a grandmother, a grandfather, an aunt or an uncle, allowing some children to be raised by a family member until they're grown and independent. The Program also focuses a great deal of attention on the child's unique strengths and educational needs. With this added attention, the child will likely experience success at school and at home. To provide greater opportunities for future success, the program has college scholarships that children can apply for when they approach college age. One former Casey child is currently in medical school.

The Casey Family Program recognizes that some foster children have known enduring, inescapable, and unalterable stresses in their lives, and that this can take its toll on otherwise healthy children. The homes they provide for these children can break the negative chain of events that may be occurring in their lives. The harmful effects of exposure to traumatizing conditions are permanently removed. The homes are designed to last.

Wraparound Services

Sometimes, children and families need very individualized types of services to stop their lives from spiraling out of control. They may need someone to come to their house to help structure the day and prepare meals, someone to provide respite to family members, someone to go to school with a child so that he gets special help at a particularly vulnerable time in his day, or someone to take a child to a recreation center after school so he can play his favorite sport or participate in his favorite activity. There are dozens of creative solutions that children, families, and service providers are capable of that create important safety nets in the lives of those who desperately need them. But most don't waste their time trying to think of them because these individualized types of services are not part of the system of care in the majority of our communities.

However, in some communities, an entirely new paradigm has emerged, known as wraparound services. Wraparound services are tailored specifically to the unique needs of children and families (VanDenBerg, 1992). Services are also often provided in the setting where they are needed the most, such as at home, at school, on the playground, or in the neighborhood. Furthermore, the services change in accordance with the changing needs of the child and family.

Creative individualized service plans are a hallmark of this new paradigm. The child who needs help moving from one task to the next in class can receive the services of a classroom helper. The parent who needs help learning how to manage a child's behavior at home can receive the services of a behavioral specialist or behavior aide, who, if necessary, can come right to the home where stresses may be the greatest. The teenager who needs to learn how to look for a job, gets a job coach. Mentoring relationships, recreation aides, respite workers, special tutors, and classroom companions are all possible. And within the wraparound model of services, funding isn't tied solely to specific programs or to specific categories of services, such as individual, group, or family psychotherapy. Flexible funding streams are created so that funds follow the child and family. This way, the service plan can change as needs change. Within a wraparound paradigm, individual risks can be targeted and needed supports can be added. For a child and family confronting multiple risks whose lives are spiraling out of control, it's now possible to design a safety net that can quickly halt and eventually reverse the trajectory.

Advocates of wraparound models also recognize that even

the most vulnerable children and families have unique strengths. They insist, therefore, that service plans highlight and help enhance a child's and family's strengths, talents, skills, and coping resources. Service plans focus more on strengths than on pathology. Another distinguishing feature is the extent to which the child's and family's natural support system is brought into the picture. Extended family members, friends, neighbors, and any other individuals felt to be an important support are not merely welcome, but sought out. This ecologically minded approach is dramatically different from what most consumers of mental health services have grown accustomed to.

Here's a brief summary of the significant differences that researchers and clinicians are highlighting between the traditional, categorical based system of care, and the individualized or wraparound model (Katz-Leavy, Lourie, Stroul, & Zeigler-Dendy, 1992; VanDenBerg, 1992).

The Assessment Process

In a categorical model, the assessment is likely to focus on pathology; dysfunction is in the spotlight. Goals are based on reducing symptoms or eliminating psychiatric diagnoses. Assessments are likely to occur at the clinic or in an office. Rarely does anyone visit the home, school, or neighborhood. The assessment is also likely conducted by a provider or team of providers who are looking at only a limited number of life areas or needs (psychological functioning, social functioning).

In a wraparound model, the assessment looks for strengths, skills, and coping resources and tries to highlight them. There is also great sensitivity to and understanding of ecological factors. What are the specific needs at home, at school, on the playground, or in the community? Providers visit the home, school, and neighborhood to understand where the vulnerabilities are and how they can best be addressed in these natural settings. Cultural and ethnic factors are carefully addressed. Family members actively participate in the assessment. Naturally occurring supports are assessed, again in the home, at school, and in the neighborhood. These supports are brought into the service plan in hopes of creating a safety net for the family. Providers have to be extremely good listeners. Naomi Tannen (1993), who helped develop a wraparound service model in Essex County, N.Y., was asked what her theoretical orientation was. Was she psychoanalytic, behavioral, eclectic? She replied that the key to their program's success wasn't based on a theoretical orientation; it was based on being able to "listen."

The Service Plan

In a categorical system of care, goals are usually tied to psychiatric diagnoses. Services are provided at a clinic or in an office. Individual, group, or family therapy sessions are usually 45 to 90 minutes, once or twice a week. In individual or group therapy, parents may play only a peripheral role and not be the focus of the plan. Goals may not necessarily be related to immediate, day-to-day needs. The expectation is that skills, strategies, and insights learned in the office will generalize to home, school, and neighborhood. Services can also come to an end for many reasons: The program may be time-limited; insurance benefits may determine the number of sessions; or symptoms may worsen, causing program providers to feel that their program is no longer appropriate.

In a wraparound model, the service plan is based more on the child's and family's needs. If symptoms or difficulties worsen, programs are not discontinued; the service plan is changed. The funding follows the child and family. If the child needs someone to guide her through afterschool recreation activities, a recreational helper can be hired. If a teenager won't get up in the morning to go to school no matter what his mother says, the plan may be to have someone come to the home to get him up and get to school. If a child's violent outbursts are making her mother feel unsafe at home, or her teacher feel unsafe at school, a home and/or school companion can be made available daily, and 'round the clock if necessary. Intensity doesn't have to mean more restrictive programming. Intensive services like the ones found in day treatment, hospital, and residential settings can instead be "wrapped around" the home, school, and neighborhood.

Agency Collaboration

Child and family needs sometimes require the involvement of more than one community service or agency. These agencies may have to work together in a coordinated fashion. When services are categorically based, this can be difficult, even though service providers may want to work together. Staffing and funding arrangements can prohibit collaboration.

Interagency collaboration, on the other hand, is a critical part of the wraparound model. Staffing and funding arrangements allow for providers from different programs to serve on the same team if a child's and family's needs require services from these different programs.

Funding Streams

In systems where services are categorically based, funds are typically tied to a specific program or clinic, which then provides services to children and families. Insurance reimbursement, when available, is tied to specific psychiatric diagnoses and to specific treatment options, such as individual therapy or hospitalization. The number of visits may be predetermined and reimbursement may be discontinued if progress is not forthcoming at a rate set by the reimbursing source.

In a wraparound model, funds follow the child and family. Services can change from benign to intensive, and back to benign, based on the child's and family's need. The child who is out of control one day can have a behavioral aide spend the entire day with her if necessary. If the aide isn't needed the next day, then the service can be discontinued. Funding isn't cut off if progress doesn't occur. Providers revise the services in accordance with persisting child and family needs.

Case Management

In a traditional system of care, the case manager or care coordinator may be the individual therapist or other provider at the clinic. The case manager's philosophy of treatment can determine the service plan, which may or may not have much to do with the child's or family's day-to-day needs. Also, service options available to the case manager are usually inflexible. In some reimbursement structures, case managers may have no regular contact with the child or family. Decisions are made based on written reports from service providers. Children and families have little to say about services that are discontinued if progress isn't occurring at a desired rate.

In a system of care based on wraparound services, the case manager or care coordinator plays a vital role in bringing together services from different points in the community to meet the child's and family's needs. The family plays an important role, working alongside the care coordinator. The process is designed to empower parents and children, to advocate for them, and ultimately to help them become their own best advocates. In some models, there's an interdisciplinary team that coordinates care, again with the family playing an integral, central role.

Currently, wraparound models are being piloted in several locations nationally, from small rural areas, to large urban settings. Schools are also implementing wraparound service models, where family members and school staff work collaboratively to design innovative, individualized programs based on need (Eber & Redditt, 1994). Families First, a wraparound model in upstate New York started by Naomi Tannen and several families, is an example of how consumers and professionals are coming together to design a new array of services that are matching up more closely with the expressed needs of parents and their children.

Families First

Tannen (1993) conducted 24 extensive interviews with parents whose children were struggling emotionally and behaviorally. Each parent was asked three simple questions: What's been helpful? What hasn't been helpful? If you had a magic wand, and could have anything that you needed, what would you want?

The parents' replies were strikingly similar; so similar, according to Tannen, that she felt she could have stopped after her tenth interview. The following is a sampling of the things that parents said they needed the most: (1) respite (2) an advocate, someone to talk to who could provide support and help make decisions about what to do for the child and family, someone who believed in them. "I wish I had someone who could just tell me what to do"; (3) information and referral. "No one ever explained to me what my child's diagnosis meant"; (4) help for brothers and sisters; (5) crisis services, such as crisis beds for cooling off periods, in-home services that are available 24 hours a day, someone who can come over and help families keep calm at any time during the day; (6) Big Brother/Big Sister for the child, a community friend, a role model; (7) a family center, that is, a central location for parent support services and services for children; and (8) concrete assistance, for example, transportation, decent housing, medical care, a telephone.

Tannen and the parents then got together and formed a

planning committee. They designed a system of care built around the things that the parents said they needed the most. The community responded very positively. Several local hotels, inns, and bed and breakfasts volunteered to provide free respite to families when they needed it. The New York State Office of Mental Health also provided funding. Private foundations contributed funds as well.

Individuals involved in Families First pay close attention to the language they use. They don't use the term "dysfunction." Tannen found that the things parents said they needed the most are things that individuals ask for when they are under great stress. "Dysfunction" has been replaced by "multistressed." Individuals involved in Families First also use "cautious" instead of "resistant"; "participant" instead of "client," and "advocate" instead of "case manager."

Two things are of paramount importance to the system of services that Tannen and the families developed. First, asking parents what they need; and second, instilling a sense of hope. Tannen (1993) feels that it is critical that people involved in the system of care believe that good things can happen.

The Interplay between Risk Exposure and Temperament

Grand Canyon tiger salamanders live in ponds along the Grand Canyon. They are insect-eating creatures who under normal circumstances don't bother each other. They swim around in the water, bag an insect from time to time, and pass the time away without much notice. When food becomes scarce however, and living conditions become overcrowded, things change. The salamanders' mouths and heads get bigger, they grow a new set of teeth, and then they begin to attack each other. Salamanders start eating other salamanders. Once conditions revert back to normal, once the stress of overcrowding

decreases, once the food supply returns to normal, the salamanders live in harmony again. Their heads shrink back to
normal size, they lose their cannibal teeth, and they start
eating insects again (Kotulak, 1993).

While we may sometimes think of our actions and reactions
as being the result of either genetic or environmental causes,
either nature or nurture, when we take a closer look, often we
can see the interaction of both (as illustrated by the Grand
Canyon tiger salamanders). This interaction differs from person to person. The stresses in one person's life may be far more
intense than those in another's; or one person might react to
stress very differently than another. One person may be better
able to adapt to stress, and may have always had this adaptive
ability, even at a very early age.

Reaction to stress is one example of how temperament can
differ among normal, healthy individuals. Temperament refers
to how we react to things in our lives. It determines our style
of behaving in the world, the way we do things and react to
things. In their ongoing longitudinal study of temperament
over the life span, Chess and Thomas (1987) note some instances where temperamental qualities stay remarkably similar
over the years, and other instances where they change.

Variations in Children's Temperament

Children will react to situations based on unique temperamental qualities that they are born with. Some children will have a
harder time than others in changing how they react to certain
situations. In addition, some may have a harder time living up
to certain rigid standards of behavior.

Children with easy temperaments, who behave predictably,
whose moods are relatively even, and who respond to new
situations well, are more likely to be involved in positive inter-
actions with others and are generally less likely to be scape-
goated. Following their exposure to some form of severe stress

or trauma, their temperament may allow them to develop a support base that can help buffer them from repeated exposure, or at least help neutralize the emotional aftereffects.

On the other hand, children who are more labile, who behave unpredictably, who react impulsively, and who don't adjust to new situations easily, are likely to meet a different fate. These children may find acceptance and understanding (things they may crave most, given their life circumstances) difficult to come by or to maintain. Their temperament increases the chances of a chain reaction of events and experiences that can further add to their pain.

By recognizing the interplay between these characteristics and a child's response to severely stressful events, it is now possible to short-circuit the predictable negative chain reaction by providing accommodations at school and at home that allow better opportunities for friendships to develop and successful experiences to be achieved.

Goodness of Fit versus Poorness of Fit

Robbie went to live with his grandparents at age 3, when his parents were sent to prison. The grandparents loved Robbie, but had difficulty managing his behavior. They also knew that they couldn't give their grandson the time he needed because of their own longstanding health and emotional problems. Both suffered from periodic bouts of depression and had drinking problems. When Robbie started school at age 5, his difficulties began to escalate. He had problems sitting still and controlling his behavior in class. Reading and spelling skills were also slow to develop because of suspected learning disabilities. At age 7, Robbie's grandparents said they could no longer manage him and Robbie went to live in a long-term foster placement.

Robbie's foster parents were very active and athletic individuals, whose energy level seemed as high as Robbie's. "We loved him from the moment we met him," they were to say years

later. Robbie's difficulties in sitting still, his difficulties in reading and spelling, and his need for extra help in managing his
behavior didn't seem that much of a deal to his foster parents.
"I was the same way when I was his age," the foster father said.
The day that Robbie went to live with this foster family was
probably the most important day in his life. He was going to
live with new parents whose temperament matched his. There
was a goodness of fit between the demands they would place
on Robbie, and his ability to meet those demands. They also
fell in love with Robbie immediately. When we speak of a
goodness of fit, we're recognizing that the demands and expectations of parents and of other important individuals in the
child's life are compatible with the child's temperamental qualities, special abilities, and other personal characteristics. When
such a fit exists, healthy development is expected (Chess &
Thomas, 1987).

Consider Robbie's fate if he had landed in the home of
foster parents who were sticklers for detail and who required
that children living in their home be able to sit perfectly still.
This would have been a poor match for Robbie, with potentially negative consequences. When we speak of poorness of
fit, we're acknowledging that the demands and expectations of
parents and other important people in the child's life are not
compatible with the child's temperamental qualities, special
abilities, and other personal characteristics. Excessive stress is
likely and healthy development is in jeopardy (Chess &
Thomas, 1987).

Temperament and Goodness of Fit
as it Relates to School

Each day that Robbie attends school, he competes with children who are better able to pay attention than he is. They're
also better able to read and write. However, Robbie is very

lucky: Not only was he placed into a new home that is very warm and nurturing, but also his new teacher at his new school is extremely understanding. She has a child of her own who has learning and attention problems and understands Robbie's frustrations in school. Robbie is protected by a teacher whose expectations match Robbie's abilities: goodness of fit. If Robbie had been placed in a classroom with a teacher who was less aware of his disabilities, and who held him accountable for things he couldn't do no matter how hard he tried, the risk of escalating out-of-control behavior would have increased dramatically. This is particularly so, given the emotional vulnerabilities that Robbie still experiences as a result of earlier losses and life stresses. Such are the consequences of a poorness of fit between a child's temperament and ability structure and a teacher's particular teaching style.

Definitions of Temperamental Categories and Constellations

Chess and Thomas's (1987) longitudinal studies have identified 9 categories of temperament, each of which can be rated as high or low:

1. *Activity level,* the motor component observed in a child's functioning. It is measured by the proportion of active versus inactive periods. The highly active child might spend a good deal of time on the playground, involved in high-energy activities; the child with a low activity level might prefer to work quietly for hours.
2. *Rhythmicity (regularity),* the predictability or unpredictability of the timing of biological functions, such as the sleep-wake cycle, hunger, feeding patterns, or bowel elimination. A child who shows regularity may awaken at the same time each morning and feel hungry at the same

time each day. A child showing irregularity can be very erratic in his or her sleeping and eating patterns.

3. *Approach or withdrawal,* the manner in which a child responds to a new situation or stimulus, whether it be a new food, a new toy, a new person, or a new place. Approach responses are positive and can be displayed by emotional expressions (smiling, verbalizing) or through motor activity (reaching for and playing with the new toy). Withdrawal reactions are negative and can also be displayed by emotional expressions (crying, fussing) or through motor activity (moving away from the new toy). The child who is high on the approach dimension may know the names of all the children in his class the first day of school. The more withdrawn child may initiate very little contact with other children in class and get to know few of them personally.

4. *Adaptability.* How does the child adapt to new situations? When placed in new and unfamiliar situations, the child who is high in adaptability may get over any initial discomfort quickly. The child who is low in adaptability can have great difficulty warming up to new situations and new routines.

5. *Sensory threshold,* the intensity of stimulation that is necessary in order to evoke a child to respond. A child with a low sensory threshold may not be able to sleep because of the way the scratchy blanket feels on his skin. Children with high sensory thresholds are much less sensitive to sensory stimuli.

6. *Intensity of reactions.* How strongly does a child respond to situations? How does the child react in situations that do not seem to be demanding, stressful, or frustrating? The parent of a child whose intensity of reactions is high might complain that her child gives up in frustration and starts yelling as soon as she thinks she can't do something. A child with low intensity can have very subdued re-

actions; she can be disappointed and others may not know it.

7. *Quality of mood,* the degree of pleasant, friendly behavior versus the amount of unpleasant, crying, and unfriendly behavior. The child whose moods are usually positive gets along easily with other people, while the child who is prone toward negative moods may have difficulty getting along and will be more likely to find something wrong with a situation or person.

8. *Distractibility,* the degree to which an outside stimulus changes the direction of a child's behavior. A child who is low in distractibility can stay focused, even when there are competing noises and distractions in the room. A child high in distractibility is easily drawn off a task by outside distractions, some of which can be very minor by other children's standards.

9. *Persistence and attention span,* the continuation of an activity despite the presence of obstacles and the length of time an activity is attended to and pursued. A child who is not persistent gives up quickly; the reverse is true for a child who has high persistence — he is likely to stick to a project after many other children have given up. A child whose attention span is short has difficulty staying focused on tasks, while a child with a long attention span can stay focused for extended periods of time.

Three Patterns of Temperament

Chess and Thomas (1993) also identified three patterns of temperament.

1. *The easy child* is the child whom everyone loves to be around. Teachers love to teach these children, coaches love to coach them in Little League. They adapt to new situations well and handle day-to-day frustrations without

much fuss. About 40% of Chess and Thomas's New York Longitudinal Study sample showed this pattern of temperament.

2. *The slow-to-warm-up child* presents a different picture. When this child is introduced into new situations or meets new people, things don't always go so smoothly. Sometimes there are negative reactions, although they are typically mild rather than intense. This child adapts slowly to change. Also, when the slow-to-warm-up child is frustrated, she may try to withdraw or pull away. Others may come to see this child as shy. About 15% of the New York Longitudinal Study sample conformed to this pattern of temperament.

3. *The difficult child.* Robert Brooks (1993) recalls a parent of a difficult child once commenting that her child made her feel like the worst parent in the world from the moment he was born. Brooks says that some of the most courageous and most motivated parents and teachers he has worked with are those who struggle day in and day out to manage and teach the difficult child. "It's like climbing Mount Everest every morning without the right equipment or training," says Brooks. "And what do these parents and teachers get for all their efforts? Often, it's criticism after criticism."

The difficult child is more prone than other children to emotional outbursts and temper tantrums. He is also prone to frequent periods of crying and takes longer to adjust to new routines. About 10% of Chess and Thomas's study sample was comprised of children who showed this pattern of temperament. And as expected, a great many parents in the study found the difficult child hard to handle.

Brooks (1993) points out that parents do not produce this specific temperamental pattern. The way parents and teachers respond, however, may minimize or maximize the difficult features of the child's behavior. Yet, add Chess and Thomas, "Given sufficient time and patient handling, these difficult children do adapt well, especially if the people and places in their world remain constant" (1987, p. 32).

There are some very effective intervention programs that seem to match up well with the needs of the difficult child, and with the needs of his or her parents and teachers. Two of these programs are the Regional Intervention Program in Nashville, Tennessee, which targets children aged 6 and under, and the Irvine Paraprofessional Program, which currently targets children in elementary school. These programs have documented their effectiveness in reducing the frequency and intensity of behavior problems in children who demonstrate hard-to-manage behaviors (Kirk, 1992; Kotkin, 1995; Strain, Steele, Ellis, & Timm, 1982; Timm, 1993). The programs are extremely cost effective and accommodate a broad range of childhood behavioral difficulties; they can also serve as a potential safety net for those families whose lives are most at risk of spiraling out of control.

THE REGIONAL INTERVENTION PROGRAM

The Regional Intervention Program incorporates effective practices for managing and controlling difficult child behaviors, and for teaching new ones. It empowers parents with the skills they need to manage their children in the years to come. What's more, the cost is minimal.

In the program, a parent works with his or her child several mornings a week over the course of several months. They work together in a room, with a staff member guiding and coaching the parent from behind a one-way mirror. The parent instructs the child to carry out different directions; the child has to listen to his parent. Since the child is there because he has problems doing what he is asked to do and controlling his behavior, it is not long before his difficulties begin to appear. The staff member teaches the parent ways of ignoring those behaviors that the parent wants to eliminate and ways of paying attention to those behaviors that the parent wants to see more of, like listening, following directions, and being able to stay in control and avoid temper outbursts.

When the child's skills begin to improve, the parent begins practicing the behavioral strategies with the child in situations where problems often occur, for example, while talking on the telephone, and conversing with friends. Those actual situations are created in the work room, and the staff member continues to coach from behind a one-way mirror in an adjacent room.

There are also other parts to the program. For example, the child spends some time in a classroom with other children, listening to a teacher, and practicing how to follow the teacher's instructions. The children are given constant feedback about their behavior and rewarded for those behaviors that need to be strengthened and learned.

The program is based on mastery. That is, the goal is to help children and parents master the skills that are necessary to reduce serious child behavioral difficulties. When the initial skills are mastered, the parent and child learn new ones. The program is not based upon attendance at a designated number of sessions or office visits, where participants may or may not learn the strategies they will need to know, and their children may or may not ultimately demonstrate the behavioral changes they want to see.

The Regional Intervention Program has also conducted follow-up studies, which showed that not only did many parents enjoy significantly improved behaviors in their children after completing the program, but also that the gains were still apparent several years later (Strain, Young, & Horowitz, 1981; Timm, 1993).

Finally, the manner in which the program recruits new staff members may represent one of its most innovative features. Parents who successfully complete the program have an option of either paying the fee or volunteering to help other parents entering the program. The staff member coaching the parent from behind the one-way mirror is a parent who successfully completed the program. This program is an illustration of people reaching out to help others who share similar needs.

THE IRVINE PARAPROFESSIONAL PROGRAM

Like the Regional Intervention Program, the Irvine Paraprofessional Program shows that it is possible to take what researchers describe as effective practices for managing and changing difficult child behaviors, like those seen in children with ADHD, and incorporate these practices into settings and situations where they are needed the most. The Irvine Paraprofessional Program incorporates these practices in school settings, specifically in regular education classrooms, before problems get to the point that special education services are needed.

A major component of the model, according to the program's director, Ron Kotkin (1994), is paraprofessionals working alongside a regular education classroom teacher. The paraprofessionals are students at the University of California, Irvine, who have completed a three-term training program leading to certification as a behavioral specialist. Once certified, they are responsible for implementing an individually designed behavioral plan for a child with ADHD who is having behavioral difficulties in class. The plan is implemented within the child's regular education classroom. The paraprofessional works very closely with the classroom teacher, serving in effect as an interim classroom aide. This way, all children in the classroom benefit from this extra support—not just the child who's receiving special help.

Conclusion

Overcoming exposure to multiple adversities can be much more difficult than overcoming one source of stress or exposure to one specific risk. Exposure to multiple risk factors or multiple sources of stress significantly increases a child's and family's chances of developing more serious problems in the future. These are the children and families most likely to experience a negative chain reaction of events in their lives and most likely to feel their lives spiraling of control. They are the ones in need of a safety net, made up of a trusted circle of support that can be there for them and, if necessary, step in and help them regain a sense of control over their lives.

In the following chapter I'll discuss pathways toward a sense of mastery—the sense that we can successfully confront challenging situations in our lives and solve difficult problems that we face. Having a sense of mastery represents another protective influence, and one that can further neutralize the potentially damaging effects of being exposed to many different hardships at once.

Chapter 8

Promoting a Sense of Mastery

The man in the cartoon looks inquisitively into the face of a small bird, who sits perched on a branch of a tree. The man asks the bird, "Do you sing because you're happy?" The bird replies, "No. I'm happy because I sing."

Having the opportunity to express our strengths, talents, and capabilities in meaningful ways, and to have them recognized and valued by the important people in our lives, helps us to define our identities around the things that we do best. Our lives are likely to be enriched emotionally as a result. These experiences will also help us to develop a sense of mastery. Mastery is the opposite of feeling helpless and hopeless. It is the feeling of being in control of one's own destiny.

The road to a sense of mastery is paved with successful experiences, successful experiences that occur over and over again in areas that are meaningful to us and to the people whom we care the most about. These experiences teach us that when we set our sights on a particular goal or a particular course of action, we'll probably get there, sooner or later. We expect to be successful if we try. If we fail, we try again, this time maybe in a different way.

Mastery can be learned (Seligman, 1995). Highlighting a child's strengths, talents, and capabilities in ways that allow important people in the child's life to recognize and value them can help a child learn to define his identity around these strengths and develop a sense of mastery. Without our help and understanding, without our ability to recognize unalterable and enduring stress, and without our willingness to provide individualized accommodations at school when they are needed, it is very difficult for a child confronting multiple risks and adversities to develop a sense of mastery.

Lavoie (1992a) once said that the world can be kinder to children with learning disabilities than schools are, because the world needs their talents. If a child does not read or spell very well, then from the first grade on there's a good chance he has defined his identity in some way around these one or two vulnerabilities. The world can also sometimes be a kinder place for traumatized children than some of our interventions have been. The world needs their strengths and talents as well. Our interventions, on the other hand, have sometimes failed to recognize that the traumatized child may express his pain through behavior rather than words.

Things are changing though. We have greater insight into childhood risks and adversities than in times past. As a result our interventions are providing vulnerable children and their families with opportunities to feel successful in situations in which they never felt successful before. One example is the following intervention involving the cooperative efforts of a school teacher and a school counselor.

Jason, an 11-year-old 6th-grader, has been dealt a very poor hand, but is courageously doing his best. For years, he was physically abused by his mother's live-in boyfriend. Although the boyfriend is no longer living with them, Jason still suffers emotionally from the experience. Jason's mother loves him very much, and Jason knows this, but she's not as available to him as much as she wishes she could be. She has a serious psychiatric illness, and has had to be hospitalized several times during the last couple of years. When she goes into the hospital it's usually for her own safety; she gets very depressed and on occasion has tried to take her own life. Jason is well aware of this also; he has seen her try to overdose on pills, and on more than one occasion he was the one to call 911 for help.

Jason is very talented in art and music, but he can't read very well. He also has difficulty staying motivated and paying attention in school. He has been diagnosed with learning disabilities and attention problems. School has been a source of great frustration, and up until his recent assessment nobody knew why. Nobody knew that he couldn't learn the way other children learn, even though he was trying harder than probably any other child in his class.

Jason's teacher and school counselor feel great compassion for Jason. They know how he has struggled through life. They also know how much he wants to be like other children, but how impossible it has been for him to enjoy the special feeling that comes from doing things well over and over again. So they decided to do something about it. Together, they are providing Jason a chance to develop a sense of mastery — something he'll need to help protect him from adverse conditions that will likely continue to surround him for some time.

There are a lot of things in Jason's life that the teacher and counselor have no control over, such as his mother's health. There are other things, though, that they do have complete control over, for example, how many experiences of success Jason will enjoy during the course of a school day, and in what areas these successes will occur. They can control this by asking Jason to participate in tasks and activities that he can master.

Jason's teacher and counselor are stacking the deck, so to

speak. Jason loves to draw houses and cars. So each day his teacher asks him to draw a picture of either a house or a car and then places the picture on the bulletin board for other children to see. Jason also loves to do small jobs for his teacher, so she made him a teacher's aide. He runs errands for her, which sometimes involve delivering messages to the school counselor.

The school counselor's job is to keep a photo album containing photographs of Jason and his accomplishments. Each week, the school counselor takes one or two Polaroid photos of Jason doing something well at school, something that he feels is meaningful. There are pictures of him drawing, running errands, and playing with his friends. There are also pictures of him trying to do things that are hard for him to do; things that show him courageously trying his best, even though he might fail, such as trying to read and spell. Under each picture in the photo album is a short story, written by the school counselor with Jason's help, describing what the picture is about, when it was taken, and how special Jason is. Every time Jason shows off his photo album, the memories of these successful experiences grow more deeply etched in his mind.

It's going to be awhile before Jason develops a real sense of mastery, but if the teacher and counselor continue their work and if others can continue the process next year and the year after, it may happen. "Life is not always a matter of holding good cards, but sometimes of playing a poor hand well." And for a child dealt a poor hand, life can take on new meaning when those who care deeply about him stack the deck.

Multiple Intelligences Theory

Thanks to the work of Howard Gardner (1993), educators, service providers, and society have become much more aware of the broad diversity of human talent. Fading rapidly is the belief that intellectual capacity can be defined by one single number or one single IQ score. There are at least seven different areas of intellectual capacity: spatial, musical, bodily kinesthetic, interpersonal, intrapersonal, linguistic, and logical-mathematical (Gardner). We vary considerably in terms of where our particular strengths lie. Some children are gifted in five of these areas, and weakest in two, linguistic and mathematical. Unfortunately, most schools focus a great deal of attention on these two areas. Children who are gifted in multiple areas, but weakest in these two are not likely to define themselves as very talented. Opportunities for developing a sense of mastery through success in other than linguistic or mathematical areas may not be as available. And if and when these successes do occur, they are not likely to be as valued.

But schools are changing. Some schools, such as the Key School in Indianapolis, Indiana, have fully integrated multiple intelligences theory into their curriculum (Blythe & Gardner, 1990). The seven areas of intelligence are stimulated every day. Children have an opportunity to express their strengths daily in a setting where these strengths are highly valued. The child whose intellectual gifts may lie within spatial or musical areas, and outside of linguistic and mathematical domains, is still seen as gifted. One's identity has a chance to form around strengths and talents rather than around areas of vulnerability. The theory of multiple intelligences may hold great promise to children who learn differently and whose identities have suffered as a result.

Fostering Emotional Strengths and Talents

There's an old Japanese tale about a belligerent samurai warrior and a Zen master. The belligerent samurai challenges the Zen master to explain the meaning of heaven and hell. The monk replies with scorn, saying that he can't waste his time with the warrior and his demands. The samurai feels attacked and flies into a rage. Removing his sword, he tells the monk that he could kill him for what he said. "That," says the Zen master, "is hell." The samurai warrior recognizes the truth in the monk's words. He sees how his rage overpowered him. "Startled at seeing the truth in what the master pointed out, the samurai calmed down, sheathed his sword, and bowed, thanking the monk for his insight." "And that," said the monk, "is heaven" (Goleman, 1995, p. 46).

We vary a great deal in our ability to express and learn from our emotions. Some of us are more willing to try again when things don't work out as expected. Some of us persist in our efforts and stay focused on our goals when things get frustrating. Some of us can control our angry feelings well enough so that they don't continually propel us into self-defeating or harmful actions. Some of us channel what we feel emotionally passionate about into activities that enhance the quality of our lives in important ways. Some of us are extremely skilled in an empathic sense. We seek greater understanding of the emotions of others in ways that strengthen our capacity to form meaningful relationships. And some of us retain a sense of hope and optimism, even during stressful times of our life.

Goleman (1995) feels that our emotional strengths and talents are often more important than our intellectual strengths and talents in determining our destiny and the quality of our lives. "Academic intelligence offers virtually no preparation for the turmoil—or opportunity—life's vicissitudes bring" (p. 36). Our emotional intelligence, he feels, will determine how well we ultimately use our other skills and talents.

Researchers have shown that children and teenagers can be taught to be more effective problem solvers, in part by becoming better skilled at identifying, understanding, expressing, and managing their emotions (Shure, 1992). They can learn to respond to challenging life circumstances actively and more confidently, and thus improve their coping skills. Often their sense of mastery also increases, and feelings of powerlessness and helplessness diminish. Garbarino (1995) advocates teaching active coping strategies such as these. He feels that children who actively seek to master emotionally challenging situations that

confront them seem to do better than those who react pas-
sively to challenges.

These strategies and skills may also be especially important to
children who have endured exposure to traumatizing conditions, and who as a result feel a sense of futurelessness. By learning how to think in terms of alternative solutions to difficult situations, children learn that they have the power to influence the
course of future events. Zimrin (1986) noted that among those
who overcame abusive childhood experiences, there was often a
strong sense of control over future events and the impact they
would have on their lives. They felt a sense of control over their
destiny. Non-survivors felt just the opposite, as though nothing
they did really mattered, so why even try.

Books and resources for teaching problem-solving strategies,
including ways to better identify, express, and manage emotions, are widely available (see appendix) for educators, counselors, therapists, or tutors. All children stand to benefit. Those
confronting major hardships, however, may need these strategies and emotional skills more than others in their attempts to
cope with the challenges they face.

These increased emotional problem solving skills may also
provide a preventive function. Goleman (1995) points out, for
example, that researchers who studied prevention models
through a multiyear project sponsored by the W.T. Grant
Foundation found that the most successful programs focused
a great deal on helping children better identify, understand,
express, and manage their emotions.

Success in Accomplishing Personally Meaningful Tasks: Required Helpfulness

It is one of the great compensations of life that no man can help
another without also helping himself.

Ralph Waldo Emerson

Individuals having to contend with stressful and dangerous situations may sometimes experience enduring positive changes in their lives when they are required to perform actions that significantly help others in their personal times of need. Rachman (1979) refers to this phenomenon as "required helpfulness." It was originally observed among the citizens of war-torn Britain during War War II. Doctors found that after aerial bombardments, citizens who served the immediate needs of others, to essentially protect the safety and well-being of others, experienced fewer than anticipated adverse psychological reactions from the trauma of the aerial assaults. One observer even noted that individuals who were of poor mental health prior to the air raids were actually faring much better following the raids if they had a personally satisfying job to perform that others saw as socially necessary (Rachman).

The phenomenon of required helpfulness has also been tested experimentally. Researchers asked a group of individuals who were very fearful of snakes to help other individuals with similar fears. By modeling effective coping strategies, the helpers actually experienced a reduction in their own fear responses (Rachman, 1979, Rakos & Schroeder, 1976).

We all need to feel that we contribute something meaningful to the world, that we make a difference, that we really matter. The act of contributing is especially important to childen with learning disabilities and attention problems. "They need to feel that they contribute something special to the world; that they make a difference" (Brooks, 1993). This feeling can be instilled in their lives by focusing on their strengths, on what Brooks calls their "islands of competence." Brooks feels that every child should be engaged in some daily activity at home and at school that allows that child to feel that he's making a contribution to the world. Activities such as tutoring another child, being a monitor at school, or taking care of a pet can provide important meaning to the life of a vulnerable child and show him that he matters.

Russell had a job that he was uniquely suited for. He supervised a group of children who were living at a residential treatment center and attending school there. Many of them were suffering from earlier exposure to severely traumatizing events in their lives. Russell had to supervise these children during recreational activities; he had to show them how to control themselves when they became frustrated or when they made a mistake. He also had to keep their spirits up and help them learn to treat one another with kindness and respect.

At the time Russell began the job, he too was living in a residential treatment program, designed to help teenagers at risk of hurting themselves. Russell had been suicidal. In fact, two weeks before he began working he tried to overdose on drugs. The staff members at his center found him and saved his life. In the days that followed the attempted suicide, the staff had to decide whether to allow Russell to begin the job that had been previously arranged for him and that they knew he very much wanted. The job matched up well with Russell's talents. He was athletic, loved helping younger children, and had the reputation of being a hard worker when given a job that he knew he could accomplish successfully.

The staff decided to let Russell have the job and to let him enjoy what they knew would be a successful experience and, more importantly, a meaningful one. Russell would be able to identify with the children he was being asked to help; he grew up under similar circumstances and had engaged in similar behaviors. He would be able to understand how these children felt.

Russell excelled at his job; he came to view it as a very significant and positive experience. His behavior and attitude changed dramatically soon after he began working. His supervisor reported that he was an excellent role model. He knew how to inspire the children he worked with and seemed to really understand their needs. Sometimes Russell pointed out specific behaviors to the children that needed correction. On occasion, he used the same expressions that staff had used when correcting his behavior in the past. Russell held his job for about seven months, until he was discharged from his residential treatment program. Prior to his discharge he won an award for being the most improved resident of the year.

Secure and Supportive Personal Relationships

There is mounting evidence that our sense of mastery and the views we maintain of ourselves can be modified by the close personal relationships that we form. Enjoying a strong emotional relationship with someone who cares deeply about our welfare can have enormous impact upon our ability to handle the hardships that we face. This is the case for all of us, regardless of age and the adversities that we confront. And it's as much true for children as it is for adults. A close emotional relationship with someone whom we care deeply about transcends any single protective influence.

Intimate relationships can go a long way in bolstering how we view ourselves and the way we are viewed by others (Rutter, 1990). For individuals who have been exposed to traumatizing conditions, the nature of their social ties and their social network can be critical to recovery. Social supports can buffer them from impending traumatic events and help them recover from those they have endured. One overcomes trauma when current attachments with safety figures outweigh the terror of the past (van der Kolk, 1994).

The number of social contacts may not be a key ingredient. Instead, it may be the quality of the relationships. Zimrin (1986) noted that individuals who successfully overcame abusive childhood experiences did not utilize a large amount of external support. What they did enjoy, however, was the benefit of a supportive relationship over time.

Goleman (1995) cites a Swedish study conducted by Annika Rosengren and others that shows the impact that a close relationship can have on our ability to handle the adversities we face. In the study, over 700 men were examined medically, and then reexamined seven years later. Each individual's level of emotional distress was also assessed. Indicators of distress included such things as going through a divorce, losing a job, experiencing financial difficulties, or being the subject of a legal action. Over the seven-year period between the two examinations, 41 of the men had died. Those who initially reported intense emotional distress in their lives had a three-times-greater chance of dying. Also, experiencing three or more significant sources of stress in the year prior to the first medical examination turned out to be a stronger predictor of dying than medical indicators such as high blood pressure or high serum cholesterol level. This was not the case, however, among individuals who enjoyed strong emotional relationships with others. Individuals who enjoyed a "dependable web of intimacy," Goleman writes, "a wife, close friends, and the like," showed no connection between high levels of emotional stress and death rate. "Having people to turn to and talk with, people who could offer solace, help and suggestions, protected them from the deadly impact of life's rigors and trauma" (p. 179).

The significantly positive influence of a supportive marriage partner was clearly apparent in the lives of those men and women raised in group homes who are now adapting well (Rutter et al., 1990). Having a supportive spouse seemed to neutralize the effects of earlier childhood adversities in the lives of these former group home residents, who were originally removed from their homes because of family breakdown.

Conclusion

A sense of mastery often develops when we successfully accomplish things that are meaningful to us and to the people whom we care most about. We learn through our experience to anticipate that our efforts will culminate in success. A sense of mastery is important in all of our lives, but it is especially important for those who have endured exposure to ongoing traumatic experiences. And that importance is magnified even further in the life of a traumatized child. "Learning to feel good about yourself is probably the single most important way that you can overcome trauma" (van der Kolk, 1994). Traumatized children who learn to feel good about themselves, who can recognize their strengths and talents, may be neutralizing the otherwise harmful long-term effects of the painful life experiences they endured.

Remember the 10-year-old child with attention deficit disorder who wrote a poem to his mother, saying over and over, "I am your son who came out as a monster?" In writing for permission from the child and his mother to use the poem at workshops and in articles and manuscripts I might write, the child's response to my request reminded me about how easy it is to overlook one's unique strengths and talents, and in so doing rob one of an opportunity to develop a sense of mastery. In the letter I sent them, I mentioned how much I was moved by the poem, and how others who read it will now know how many children with similar learning and attention problems sometimes feel and how many adults with these disabilities felt when they were children. In the letter I also mentioned that I would keep the child's name confidential. A week or so later, I received permission from both the child's mother and the child. But the child scribbled a little note to me under his name: "Use my name. It's my poem. I want credit."

Of course he does. He is a gifted writer who has a unique talent when it comes to communicating his thoughts and feelings. Thanks, Joshua. You're a great writer. Thanks to you and your family for sharing your poem. It has moved many of us who have read it.

In the next chapter, I will discuss the phenomenon of turning point experiences and second-chance opportunities, their influence in the lives of those who have overcome adverse childhood conditions, and ways that some have been provided with access to these experiences and opportunities.

Chapter 9

Turning Points
and Second-Chance
Opportunities

Most of us who work in one of the helping professions think that vulnerable children who become strong, successful adults make their successful transition slowly, over many years, as a result of the treatment interventions that they received or school programs that they participated in. In some instances this may be true. But there are many individuals whose turning points occurred as a result of very different experiences. Sometimes their lives turned around quickly. And the changes happened much later in their lives than many would have expected, and later than some would have thought possible.

Rutter (1990) and Werner (1993, 1995) speak of life's turning points — when new experiences, situations, or relationships create opportunities for change. This change can sometimes dramatically alter how we view ourselves in relation to others. In turn, it can also alter our future development. Starting school can be a turning point. It offers exposure to new tasks and new relationships. If the experiences are handled successfully, school can serve as a protective influence or a buffer for children who suffer from the pain of earlier trauma or enduring stresses in their lives. Failure in school, on the other hand, can serve to increase the pain, add to the stress, and heighten the risk for serious difficulties during later stages of life.

Later in childhood, the opportunity to express and cultivate a unique talent or a specific interest such as music, art, or sports, may represent a potential turning point. Many individuals cite childhood interests and talents that they were allowed to develop and express as very important in helping them develop a sense of confidence in their abilities.

Turning point experiences occur throughout the lifespan. Some individuals identify one event, one relationship, one experience as a turning point. Others identify several. Some say that positive changes occurred quickly. Others say they occurred slowly, over time. Some individuals identify a special enduring relationship that they developed with someone whom they came to love deeply. Other individuals identify their careers or their involvement in military service as a turning point. Some speak of a spiritual awakening that occurred, where a new view of themselves emerged. And some individuals cite an unexpected chance encounter that brought a new and important person into their lives and permanently altered their life course.

Chance encounters are unintended meetings involving individuals who never met each other before. Chance encounters often have little, if any, long-term effects on our lives. But every now and then a fortuitous and sometimes very brief meeting with someone leaves us with a new way of looking at things. We take from this brief meeting valuable new knowledge or new future options.

Bill Clinton's trip from Arkansas to Washington, D.C., at age 16 was a turning point experience in his life. During that trip, he met John F. Kennedy. The meeting couldn't have lasted more than a few seconds. A picture was taken of their meeting, which Bill Clinton took back to Arkansas with him, and reportedly has treasured ever since. If one listens closely to some of Clinton's speeches, and even watches some of his mannerisms, John Kennedy's influence is clear. Could a brief meeting with John Kennedy decades earlier have had this type of profound influence on his life? Could that one brief meeting represent such a monumental turning point experience? Researchers who study the ways in which individuals overcome earlier adversities in their lives do in fact speak of turning point experiences happening in this way. Sometimes they unfold over an extended period of time. And sometimes turning point experiences occur very quickly, by virtue of brief chance encounters.

During President Clinton's trip to Russia in 1994, he held a town hall meeting with Russian journalists and students, which was broadcast live around the world. During the meeting, Russian citizens were given the opportunity to ask the President of the United States a variety of questions. From the back of the room, a 13-year-old boy raised his hand and asked Clinton how old he was when he went to Washington and shook John Kennedy's hand. Bill Clinton answered that he was 16 years old. He then asked the child to join him on stage. "Come here. Come shake hands with me and maybe you'll become President of Russia someday." Clinton placed his arm around the child's shoulder, shook his hand, and talked about the time he met President Kennedy, telling the child that it was around that time that he knew he wanted to go into public service.

For many people, this brief exchange represented a warm

and tender moment. The incident, however, was then likely soon forgotten. But for those who study life's trajectories, and particularly the way in which individual lives change for the positive in response to fortuitous encounters, this brief exchange was not soon forgotten. It may represent a turning point experience in the life of a 13-year-old Russian boy. He may not grow up to be President of Russia, but he may someday achieve heights he would not have achieved had this chance encounter not occurred.

Creating Access to Turning Points and Second-Chance Opportunities

Some people have greater access to turning point experiences and therefore may be offered greater protection than others (Rutter, 1990). For example, being skilled academically may allow you to get to college, which may allow access to a certain career path, which may represent your turning point. The child whose academic skills were never enriched and who had limited chances for expressing special interests and talents does not have the same access to turning point experiences.

The "I Have A Dream" Foundation

The "I Have A Dream" Foundation, started by Eugene Lang, provides an opportunity for a college education to students who otherwise might not see this as a reachable goal. Lang, now a successful businessman, attended Public School 121 in East Harlem, New York City, as a child. In 1981, he returned to his old school to give a speech. During his speech, he promised the 6th-grade class that if they graduated high school with satisfactory grades, and if they stayed away from behaviors that would jeopardize their futures, he would pay for their college education. Lang, along with volunteers and counselors, were available to the students in the years that followed to encourage them and to help them if necessary.

Of the 51 students that Lang agreed to support in 1981, 47 earned their high school diplomas or GED. Approximately 90% are expected to complete at least 2 years of college. Over the past several years, business leaders in other communities have been replicating the "I Have A Dream" program (National Commission on Children, 1991).

Before Lang's speech in 1981, many people visiting Public School 121 would not have envisioned these children in college someday. The "I Have A Dream" Foundation provided an opportunity for turning point experiences to occur in these children's lives.

School as a Turning Point

Creating a goodness of fit between a child's strengths and talents and an environment that recognizes and values these strengths and talents, opens up opportunities for turning point experiences to occur. Walk into any classroom in any city and ask the students to draw you a picture of a house. At least one of those pictures will likely grab you. You'll look at the picture and say, "This child could be an architect." You're right. But if the child can't spell or read very well, then there's a good chance that his identity has likely already formed around his one or two vulnerabilities. And if this has happened, he probably sees himself as stupid. He's got the makings of an architect but doesn't know it; he may never become an architect. The odds change, however, if he finds himself in a setting that values one's capacity to draw houses. The odds really change if he meets and gets to know an architect who recognizes and nurtures his unique talent.

Schools that are incorporating Gardner's (1993) theory of multiple intelligences into their curriculum may be opening up turning point opportunities for children and teenagers. Students whose talents lie in spatial areas, students who are musically gifted, and students who possess unusual tactile-kinesthetic strengths can have their talents nourished and nurtured. These gifts and talents are valued. One's identity now has a chance of forming around them.

Stories of Turning Point Experiences

The stories that follow are of turning point experiences and second chance opportunities in the lives of those who have endured a hurtful past. As children, they were exposed to enduring and inescapably painful conditions that they couldn't alter no matter how hard they tried. They know this now, and seem stronger as a result.

24-year-old Kenneth is working full time and trying to save up enough money to send himself through four years of college. He was recently accepted to a well-known university and anticipates starting school next fall. He is happy with his life, sees himself as strong and independent, and enjoys close and supportive relationships with others. Kenneth's life started out much differently. He was abused by his mother and abandoned at age 7. Things soon changed for the better, though, when, also at age 7, Kenneth was placed in a long-term group home facility. Staff members at the facility noticed that he was unable to hear very well. His hearing was checked and in fact he did have a significant hearing loss. Kenneth was fitted with a hearing aide, which allowed him to hear sounds that he never heard before. This, says Kenneth, was a turning point experience in his life.

Kenneth talks about a second turning point experience, which occurred while he was in high school. One day he noticed a flyer on a bulletin board announcing a meeting for

American students wanting to study overseas. He liked the idea of studying abroad, and of seeing different places. Kenneth attended the meeting. Looking back, he now sees it as another turning point in his life. Kenneth saw what it would take to study abroad and he set his sights on accomplishing that. Within a relatively short period of time, his dream was realized. He spent a year attending school in Europe. That year abroad allowed him to see his life in a new way. It gave him some distance from the earlier painful experiences he had endured and provided him with a new, more optimistic and hopeful perspective. Kenneth also says that he gained a great deal of confidence from that year. He was treated by those he met as adventurous. They admired his independence and take-charge spirit. He soon began to admire these same qualities in himself.

Sonja is 22 years old and attends a major four-year university in the midwest. She sees herself as independent and success-ful, and so do those who know her well. Sonja has set some lofty career goals for herself, which she and those who know her feel that she'll accomplish. She has a history of accomplish-ing things that she sets out to do. Earlier on in Sonja's life, though, things didn't look very promising.

Sonja was born to very poor parents. As a child, she was also sexually abused. Authorities eventually placed her in foster care for her own safety, and also because her parents refused to care for her anymore. For a period of time, Sonja went from foster home to foster home. Her turning point experience occurred when she was placed with foster parents who com-mitted themselves to her in a way that hadn't happened in any of her previous foster placements. These foster parents would care for Sonja as though she was their own child, and they would provide a home for her until she was ready to live on her own.

Sonja always showed enormous strength in the face of difficult life circumstances. What she lacked were the opportunities provided to other children growing up under safer and more hopeful conditions. Her new foster parents would now provide her with these opportunities. They would also offer her stability and security. Sonja got the home she needed. Her foster parents also helped her apply for a four-year college scholarship, which she eventually received. Sonja is doing well in her studies and anticipates enjoying a bright and hopeful future.

John feels that the military service provided him with an important turning point experience in his life. John is in his early 30s, and doing well. He is married, the father of a 6-year-old daughter, and an officer in the navy. His currently successful life adjustment is a very far cry from how he functioned in his younger years. Briefly, John was placed in a residential treatment facility at age 7. He was unable to control his behavior, and his parents felt that for his own protection, and the protection of others, he should be placed in residential care. Despite the intensive treatment that he received in this facility, his problems persisted after his discharge. He eventually went to live in a group home, where to continued to reside well into his adolescence. While living in the group home, he was molested by one of the male house parents. John eventually ran away. He got into drugs, lost contact with his family, and drifted around the country. As a young adult, he tried to enter the armed services, but was turned down. He tried again several years later, and was accepted. He loved basic training. He loved wearing his uniform and the structure that military life provided him. A few months into his first tour of duty, he met the woman he would marry, a chance encounter that would prove to be another turning point experience in John's life. She knew only that he was a strikingly handsome man who was proud to be in the military. When she learned of the painful things that John endured as a child and teenager, she marveled

at his strength and at how resilient he was to be able to overcome these experiences. John came to view himself the same
way.

Steve is 40 years old, very creative, and part owner of a
successful record company that has signed some well-known
rock groups. He feels that his life is going well, and he recognizes that with hard work he can generally accomplish the
goals that he sets for himself. Steve also has learning disabilities. He remembers when he was a child, of feeling humiliated
by not being able to read and spell words the way that his
classmates could. Steve remembers the fear he experienced
sitting in class, waiting to be called upon. To this day, he looks
back upon these experiences as some of the most difficult and
terrorizing moments that he has known.

Things changed for Steve in 7th grade, when his parents
sent him to a new school. The new school stressed a different
set of skills and talents and paid a great deal of attention to
abstract intellectual matters. Steve was extremely creative and
inventive; the school recognized and fostered these areas of
talent.

Steve sees his transfer to this new school as a turning point
in his life. For the first time he experienced what it felt like to
be successful at school. Steve began to see himself differently.
He no longer saw himself as incapable of achieving things; he
began to recognize that he had strengths and talents. He now
knew that there were areas in which he could compete successfully with other students.

Cynthia is 43 years old and works full time as a probation
officer. She is the mother of two teenagers, a 14-year-old son
and a 12-year-old daughter. She and her ex-husband divorced
several years ago, and currently remain close friends, sharing
the responsibility for raising their two children. Cynthia has an
attention deficit disorder, which has affected her throughout

her life. During all her years in school, Cynthia always thought of herself as unintelligent. When she did things well she felt that she was just lucky. When things didn't turn out as she had hoped, it made sense; it fit her opinion of herself and her abilities. She was absolutely convinced that she was far less intelligent and capable than others. This conviction stayed with her until the day she was sitting in a psychologist's office, listening to him discuss her son's test results. Cynthia's son was having problems in school that were similar to the ones she experienced. The psychologist assessed Cynthia's son and described for her the nature of his difficulties. He talked about her son's many intellectual talents, his broad interests in science, and he talked about how hard it was for her son to stay motivated and focused in class. Cynthia's son was diagnosed with attention deficit disorder, a term that Cynthia had heard before, but one she knew very little about. As she heard the psychologist describe her son's areas of strength and areas of vulnerability, she knew he was also talking about her. She had the same strengths and vulnerabilities. Cynthia finally had an explanation for why she did some things so well and why she had such difficulty doing others; other things that for most people can be so easy to do, like remembering directions, organizing activities, or completing projects and tasks. Cynthia describes that meeting with the psychologist as a turning point experience in her life. It gave her the words to validate feelings that she had been experiencing for 40 years. She has since gone on to advocate for other adults who experienced similar years of frustration and failure in school.

"The day I turned my life over to God," says Raymond, "was the day my life changed." Raymond is the director of a recreation center in Southern California. He supervises several staff members and is seen as one of the best recreation program directors in the area. Earlier in his life, though, Raymond struggled. School was very difficult for him. He was suspended on a few different occasions. There were also problems at home. "At least two nights a week," says Raymond, "my father would come home drunk and out of his mind. . . . On some of those nights, he beat me and my brother pretty bad . . . and sometimes he'd beat my mom pretty bad too." Raymond says that the last two years of high school were the worst years of his life. "I ran around with a really tough group of kids and we got into a lot of trouble." Raymond spent over a year in a residential treatment facility, and was discharged on his 18th birthday.

Raymond had few people he felt he could turn to or really trust. He was hurting real bad and on a few occasions contemplated killing himself. There was one person he always liked and trusted, though: the pastor at his church. Raymond used to go to church with his parents when he was much younger, but he hadn't gone for years. He wondered whether the pastor was still there. And if he was, whether he would even remember him.

It turned out the pastor was still there, and he remembered Raymond very well. They quickly renewed their earlier friendship and close bond. Raymond spent a lot of time at the pastor's church and with the pastor's family at home. Eventually a job opened up as a youth counselor in the church's school. Raymond got the job.

During that period of his life, Raymond experienced a spiritual rebirth. He doesn't talk about it that much, other than to the pastor, but he feels that this spiritual reawakening led to important changes in his life. "I've turned my life over to God. I don't worry about the things I used to worry about; I know that things will work out. It's in God's hands."

The last story is also of a life transformed by a spiritual rebirth. The storyteller prefers to remain anonymous and to convey the essence of his turning point experience through the words of a poem by Myra B. Welch (1993), "The Touch of the Master's Hand."

'Twas battered and scarred, and the auctioneer
Thought it scarcely worth his while
To waste much time on the old violin,
But held it up with a smile.
"What am I bidden, good folks," he cried,
"Who'll start the bidding for me?"
"A dollar, a dollar," then, two! Only two?
"Two dollars, and who'll make it three?
"Three dollars, once; three dollars, twice;
Going for three . . . " But no,
From the room, far back, a grey-haired man
Came forward and picked up the bow;
Then, wiping the dust from the old violin,
And tightening the loose strings,
He played a melody pure and sweet
As a caroling angel sings.

The music ceased, and the auctioneer,
With a voice that was quiet and low,
Said: "What am I bid for the old violin?"
And he held it up with the bow.
"A thousand dollars, and who'll make it two?
Two thousand! And who'll make it three?
Three thousand, once; three thousand, twice;
And going and gone," said he.

The people cheered, but some of them cried,
"We do not quite understand
What changed its worth?" Swift came the reply:
"The touch of a master's hand."

And many a man with life out of tune,
And battered and scarred with sin,
Is auctioned cheap to the thoughtless crowd,
Much like the old violin.

> A *"mess of potage,"* a glass of wine;
> A game-and he travels on.
> He is *"going"* once, and *"going"* twice,
> He's *"going"* and almost *"gone."*

> But the Master comes and the foolish crowd
> Never can quite understand
> The worth of a soul and the change that's wrought
> By the touch of the Master's hand.

Conclusion

The 1980s and 1990s have seen a proliferation of books and articles related to different environmentally-based childhood risks and adversities. Much has been written on the effects of child physical abuse, child sexual abuse, growing up poor, and exposure to different forms of violence. There has also been a proliferation of books and articles related to two of the most common neuropsychologically-based childhood conditions: attention deficit disorder and learning disabilities.

Surprising little attention, however, has been given to how people actually overcome these different adversities. There has been a great deal of attention given to treatments for these different conditions, but that's a different discussion and an important distinction. It implies that these conditions are overcome primarily through existing categories of treatment, of which seven comprise almost the entire system of mental health care in many communities: individual therapy, family therapy, group therapy, day treatment, hospitalization, residential treatment, and special school programs. Undoubtedly, the different categories of treatment that many successful adults received was instrumental in helping them through very difficult childhood experiences. But if we listen to researchers studying how people overcome childhood adversities, it is clear that there are many potential turning points, and if we focus on specific categories of treatment we may never notice the turning points. The findings are very compelling, and have enormous implications for those who have endured traumatizing childhood experiences or whose learning difficulties during their school years robbed them of a sense of mastery.

Each of the programs mentioned in Part III provided an illustration of how one particular protective influence could be incorporated into the lives of vulnerable children and families. In reality, these programs are capable of incorporating many sources of protection. The Casey Family Program offers long-term foster home care to children until they're adults and ready to live independently; it can provide access to all of the protective influences that we have discussed. Families First is a wraparound model that is also capable of incorporating several protective processes into the lives of children and families. The same can be said for the Regional Intervention Program, the Irvine Paraprofessional Program, and the "I Have a Dream" Foundation.

Many other impressive programs and services with similar capabilities could also have been mentioned here. Communities throughout the country are piloting innovative, collaborative models that are addressing the multiple needs of vulnerable children, families, and adults in creative, new ways. These efforts are looking beyond fixed categories of treatment to a new array of flexible and individualized services.

Protective influences exist within us, within our families and within our communities (Werner, 1995). Together, these protective influences can outweigh the effects of exposure to a range of childhood risks. Educators and health care providers working side by side with caring individuals who comprise one's special circle of support can collectively make these protective influences available to those who need them most; pro-

tective influences that researchers say can outweigh the effects
of a variety of different risk factors and adverse conditions.

And by attending to protective influences such as these,
we'll begin to see child and family needs in a very different
light. We'll acknowledge that certain risks can persist for many
years, and, as such, children and families may need to be
shielded and protected in special ways for many years. We'll
adopt a lifespan perspective. And our notion of intervention
will extend well beyond narrow professional disciplines. New
importance will be placed on neighborhood resources that can
shield children during afterschool hours. Schools will be evaluated for their protective value, knowing that some will buffer
children better than others. Individuals who family members
look up to, and who are part of their circle of support, will take
on very special significance. Added recognition will be given to
the role that mentoring relationships can play. A child's unique
strengths and talents will take on special importance, since
their expression will be seen as key to developing a sense of
mastery and confidence. We'll always be on alert for new resources and materials that help children and families reframe
adversities in a new way; that give them the words they'll need
to validate and legitimize the pain they've endured. And we'll
remain continually focused on the need to reinstill a sense of
hope in the lives of children and families who feel futureless,
who have given up trying to alter conditions and circumstances
that may indeed be unalterable if they do not have access to
new sources of protection, strength, and understanding.

Check out " Within our Reach\ Breaking the
        cycle of Disadvantages" by
                    Lisbeth Schorr.

Appendix: Resources

Understanding the Effects of Exposure to Traumatic Experiences

Understanding Psychological Trauma
    Part I: Learning from Survivors
    Part II: Healing and Recovery
    Part III: Healing Our Children (Tape 1: Symptomatology; Tape 2: Assessment; Tape 3: Treatment)
    Baxley Media Group, 110 West Main Street, Urbana, Illinois 61801; phone: 217-384-4838; fax: 217-384-8280 (5 videotapes)

Together, these five videotapes offer a comprehensive and compassionate overview of the effects of psychological trauma on adults and on children. Parts I and II portray adults who

have overcome traumatic life experiences. As they recount
their stories, viewers gain greater insight into the consequences
of exposure to traumatic events, and ways of healing from the
experience. Part III is entirely dedicated to childhood trauma.
Three separate videotapes provide viewers with a greater understanding of the effects of traumatization of children by the
very individuals they look to for safety and protection.

Four Men Speak Out
Varied Directions International, 69 Elm Street, Camden,
Maine 04843; phone: 800-888-5236 (video)

Four men who were sexually abused as children recount
their abuse experience. They discuss how the experience has
affected them emotionally, and what steps they took, and continue to take, in order to heal. Viewers see the diverse effects
that child sexual abuse can have on male survivors. Viewers
also become more aware of why males often don't disclose
earlier abusive experiences.

Why Does Mom Drink So Much?
Human Relations Media, 175 Tompkins Avenue, Pleasant-
ville, New York 10570; phone: 800-431-2050; fax: 914-747-1744
(video)

School-age children talk to alcohol treatment counselors
about what life is like living with an alcoholic parent. Their
silence is broken, their secret is out, and they learn that it is
not their fault. The counselors provide valuable knowledge to
these children, and to viewers on the nature of alcoholism,
how it can affect all family members, and what each member
can do to improve the quality of their lives.

Kids with Courage: True Stories about Young People Making a Difference
Barbara A. Lewis, 1992, Free Spirit Publishing, Inc., 400 First Avenue North, Suite 616, Minneapolis, Minnesota 55401; phone: 612-338-2068 (book)

Children and teenagers who overcame adversities in their lives tell their stories, in hopes that the reader can learn from their experiences. The book also contains true stories of kids engaged in social action programs designed to help other kids and their communities. A teacher's guide accompanies the book in order to help teachers apply these stories to a class-room setting.

Let's Talk about Living in a World with Violence: An Activity Book for School-Age Children
James Garbarino, 1993, Erikson Institute, 420 North Wa-bash Avenue, Chicago, Illinois 60611; phone: 312-755-2250 (workbook)

This workbook offers children exposed to violence a way to better understand what they are seeing and what they are having to endure. It also provides activities that they can do to help them feel better and enjoy more peace in their lives. The workbook relies on the guidance of a caring adult who can take children through the various activities. Guidebooks are provided for parents, teachers, and counselors that show how the exercises and activities contained in the workbook can be used in meaningful ways.

Understanding Learning Disabilities

Understanding Learning Disabilities: How Difficult Can This Be? The F.A.T. City Learning Disability Workshop

Richard D. Lavoie, 1989, P.B.S. VIDEO, 1320 Braddock Place, Alexandria, Virginia 22314; phone: 800-424-7963 (video)

Richard Lavoie takes a group of professionals and parents of learning disabled children through a simulation exercise designed to show adults what it feels like to be a child with a learning disability. The effects are often very powerful. Viewers come away with a new understanding of learning disabilities, and how they can affect children, particularly when they go undetected.

Reach for the Stars: An Inspiring Story for People with Learning Disabilities
Joy Galane, Editor, 1985, The Lab School of Washington, 4759 Reservoir Road, NW, Washington, DC 20007; phone: 202-965-6600 (video)

Each year, the Lab School of Washington presents awards to well-known figures who have achieved great success in their particular field, in spite of having learning disabilities. Award winners come to the Lab School to receive their awards and to share their personal stories with the learning disabled students currently attending the school. This video shows the 1985 award winners, who included Tom Cruise, Cher, and Bruce Jenner. The message to viewers of this video is that success is not out of the reach of children and adults with learning disabilities.

Color Me Successful: The Outstanding Learning Disabled Achievers Honored by the Lab School of Washington
The Lab School of Washington, 1993, 4759 Reservoir Road Northwest, Washington, DC 20007; phone: 202-965-6600 (coloring book)

The pages of this coloring book contain photographs of famous people with learning disabilities. The individuals in the

"*Reach for the Stars*" video (above) are represented, as are over 20 others. Under each photograph is a line drawing related in some fashion to the contribution or achievement of the famous person in the photograph. The drawing can be colored in by children. Individuals highlighted in the book are well-known figures from all walks of life, including scientists, politicians, physicians, athletes, artists, actors, and others. These very different individuals share one important feature in common: they all have learning disabilities.

Different is Not Bad, Different is the World
Sally Smith, 1994, Sopris West, 1140 Boston Avenue, Longmont, Colorado 80501; phone: 303-651-2829 (book)

Smith is Director and Founder of the Lab School of Washington, DC. This books is intended to help children with disabilities understand that everyone is different; we all have things that we are good in and things that we are not as good in. The book is colorfully illustrated and sensitively written. It can help all readers understand that we are all different in how we live and learn.

Understanding Attention Deficit Disorder

The A.D.D. WareHouse
300 Northwest 70th Avenue, Plantation, Florida 33317; phone: 800-233-9273

The A.D.D. WareHouse specializes in books, videos, and other products related to attention deficit disorder. Some of the videos they distribute that help parents and teachers better understand the nature of A.D.D. include "*Why Won't My Child Pay Attention*" and "*Educating Inattentive Children,*" both by Sam Goldstein, Ph.D., and Michael Goldstein, M.D. Among

the books they distribute that help children better understand
A.D.D. are *"Jumpin' Johnny Get Back to Work: A Child's Guide
to ADHD/Hyperactivity"* and *"I Would If I Could: A Teenager's
Guide to ADHD/Hyperactivity,"* both by Michael Gordon,
Ph.D. A third publication by Gordon, titled *"My Brother's a
World-Class Pain,"* is intended to help siblings of children with
A.D.D.

New videos and books are always being added to the A.D.D.
Warehouse catalogue, many of which provide the most current
findings on how to best help children, adults, and families
struggling with attention related difficulties.

Teaching Problem Solving Skills to Children

The following resources may provide useful information and
curricula for those wishing to teach children and teenagers
how to be more effective problem solvers.

*I Can Problem Solve: An Interpersonal Cognitive Problem
Solving Program*
Myrna B. Shure, 1992, Research Press, Department 96, PO
Box 9177, Champaigne, Illinois 61821; phone: 217-352-3273

Based on research showing that children can learn the specific skills necessary to be better problem solvers, the author
developed a series of lesson plans designed to teach children
these important skills. Lessons teach children, among other
things, how to better understand and label feelings, how to
better understand the feelings and perspective of others, how
to better understand the relationship between one's behavior
and its effect on others, how to better identify problems before
they occur, and how to think about different ways of solving
problems. The lessons and activities are designed for teachers
to use in the classroom. Teachers are provided with a guide-

book that illustrates ways to use the lesson plans, along with ideas of how to adapt the lessons and activities to different student needs.

The Prepare Curriculum: Teaching Prosocial Competencies
Arnold P. Goldstein, 1988, Research Press, Department 96, PO Box 9177, Champaign, Illinois 61821; phone: 217-352-3273

This is a comprehensive resource book. Goldstein reviews, in detail, a range of different psychoeducational programs and curricula and describes programs that teach problem solving skills, social skills, anger management skills, as well as various other prosocial competencies. While many of the programs were designed for children with specific deficits in these areas, the programs are, in actuality, capable of enhancing the prosocial skills of all children.

Conflict Resolution: An Elementary School Curriculum
Gail Sadala, Meg Holmberg, and Jim Holligan, 1990, Conflict Resolution Resources For Schools and Youth, The Community Board Program, 149 Ninth Street, San Francisco, California 94103; phone: 415-863-6100; 415-552-1250

For teachers who wish to help their students learn better ways to handle everyday conflicts, the authors developed an entire curriculum around conflict resolution. Lessons and activities help students become more aware of everyday conflicts and alternative ways of handling them. Lessons and activities cover such skill areas as understanding individual differences and different points of view, understanding, recognizing and describing feelings, learning how to talk to another person about a conflict and the power of listening.

Learning to Be a Healthy Kid
Lyn Perino and Justin Cunningham, 1992, San Diego
County Office of Education and the California State Depart-
ment of Education, San Diego County Office of Education,
Graphics Communications, Room 212, 6401 Linda Vista Road,
San Diego, California 92111-7399; phone: 619-292-3724

This curriculum was developed by a team of educators in
California that uses literature as a vehicle for helping children
understand the concept of resilience. Award-winning and high-
interest books were selected, ranging from historical fiction to
autobiographies. Activities encourage expressive writing, in-
depth discussions, and family-school participation. In selecting
publications and activities, particular attention and sensitivity
was paid to the culturally diverse backgrounds of California
school children. The curriculum, which includes themes and
lessons that encompass literature, language arts, history, and
social science, was designed for grades 3, 4, and 5. The authors
felt that prevention programs such as this one may yield their
greatest gains if implemented during these grade levels.

Resilience through the Lifespan

Learning Development Services, in San Diego, Ca., started the
"Resilience through the Life Span" project in an effort to learn
more about how individuals overcome a range of different
childhood adversities. Individuals who overcame adverse conditions in their earlier years, and who wish to participate in the
project, are asked if their stories can be videotaped. They are
also asked for permission to show these videotapes to children,
families, or others who might be able to learn from their experiences. Individuals participating in the project are asked four
questions: What have you learned? As you look back, what
were some of the strengths that you feel you had, or that you

developed, that helped you through the tough times? Were there any turning point experiences that you can remember, which led to things changing for the better? Based on what you've learned, what would you tell young people who are going through what you went through?

Anyone interested in participating in the project, please write to Learning Development Services Resilience Project, 3754 Clairemont Drive, San Diego, California 92117; phone: 619-276-6912; fax: 619-483-3567

References

Amaya-Jackson, L., Mesco, R. H., McGough, J. J., & Cantwell, D. P. (1992, Summer). Attention-deficit/hyperactivity disorder. In E. Peschel, R. Peschel, R. C. W. Howe, & J. W. Howe (Eds.), *Neurobiological disorders in children and adolescents* (pp. 45–50). San Francisco: Jossey-Bass.

American Psychiatric Association. (1994). *Diagnostic and statistical manual of mental disorders* (4th ed.). Washington, DC: Author.

Anthony, J. (1985). Resilience in children. *The Psychiatric Times, 2*(4), 13–14.

Baldwin, A. L., Baldwin, C., & Cole, R. E. (1990). Stress-resistant families and stress-resistant children. In J. Rolf, A. S. Masten, D. Cicchetti, K. H. Nuechterlein, & S. Weintraub (Eds.), *Risk and protective factors in the development of psychopathology* (pp. 257–280). New York: Cambridge University.

Barkley, R. (1990). *Attention-deficit/hyperactivity disorder: A handbook for diagnosis and treatment.* New York: Guilford.

Barkley, R. (1994, October). *It's about time.* Keynote presentation at the sixth annual conference of CH.A.D.D. (Children and Adults with Attention Deficit Disorder), New York.

Barocas, R., Seifer, R., & Sameroff, A. J. (1985). Defining environmental risk: Multiple dimensions of psychological vulnerability. *American Journal of Community Psychology, 13*(4), 433–447.

Beardslee, W., & Podorefsky, D. (1988). Resilient adolescents whose parents have serious affective and other psychiatric disorders: Importance of self understanding and relationships. *American Journal of Psychiatry, 145,* 63–68.

Bleuler, M. (1978). *The schizophrenic disorders: Long-term patient and family studies.* New Haven: Yale University.

Bleuler, M. (1984). Different forms of childhood stress and patterns of adult psychiatric outcome. In N. S. Watt, E. J. Anthony, L. C. Wynne, & J. E. Rolf (Eds.), *Children at risk for schizophrenia: A longitudinal perspective* (pp. 537–542). New York: Cambridge University.

Blythe, T., & Gardner, H. (1990, April). A school for all intelligences. *Educational Leadership,* 33–37.

Brooks, R. (1993, October). *Fostering the self-esteem of children with ADD: The search for islands of competence.* Presentation at the fifth annual conference of CH.A.D.D. (Children and Adults with Attention Deficit Disorder), San Diego.

Carnegie Council on Adolescent Development. (1994). *A matter of time: Risk and opportunity in the out of school hours.* New York: Carnegie Corporation of New York.

Chess, S., & Thomas, A. (1987). *Know your child: An authoritative guide for today's parents.* New York: Basic.

Cohen, S., & Wills, T. A. (1985). Stress, social support and the buffering hypothesis. *Psychological Review, 98*(2), 310–357.

Doyle, J. S., & Bauer, S. K. (1989). Post-traumatic stress disorder in children: Its identification and treatment in a residential setting for emotionally disturbed youth. *Journal of Traumatic Stress, 2*(3), 275–288.

Eber, L., & Redditt, C. A. (1994, March). *Restructuring service models and shifting roles: An approach for systems change.* Presentation at the seventh annual Research Conference for Children's Mental Health, Tampa, FL.

Fahlberg, V. (1995, April). *Attachment and resiliency.* Presentation at the Conference on Resiliency in Children and Families. Helena, Montana: Intermountain Children's Home, Casey Family Program, and the Summit Project.

Famularo, R., Kinscherff, R., & Fenton, T. (1992). Psychiatric diagnoses of maltreated children: Preliminary findings. *Journal of the American Academy of Child and Adolescent Psychiatry, 31*(5), 863–867.

Fitzwater, I. (1990). *Laugh with me/cry with me.* San Antonio: Watercress.

Frankl, V. (1963). *Man's search for meaning: An introduction to logotherapy.* New York: Washington Square.

Freedman, M. (1993). *The kindness of strangers.* San Francisco: Jossey-Bass.

Gabel, S., Finn, M., & Ahmad, A. (1988). Day treatment outcome with severely disturbed children. *Journal of the American Academy of Child and Adolescent Psychiatry, 4,* 479–482.

Garbarino, J. (1993). *Let's talk about living in a world with violence: An activity book for school-age children.* Chicago: Erikson Institute.

Garbarino, J. (1994, August). *Children living in a violent world.* Presentation at the 102nd annual meeting of the American Psychological Association, Los Angeles, CA.

Garbarino, J. (1995). *Raising children in a socially toxic environment.* San Francisco: Jossey-Bass.

Garbarino, J., Dubrow, N., Kostelny, K., & Pardo, C. (1992). *Children in danger: Coping with the consequences of community violence.* San Francisco: Jossey-Bass.

Garbarino, J., Kostelny, K., & Dubrow, N. (1991). What children can tell us about living in danger. *American Psychologist, 46*(4), 376–383.

Gardner, H. (1993). *Multiple intelligences: The theory in practice.* New York: Basic.

Garmezy, N. (1991). Resiliency and vulnerability to adverse developmental outcomes associated with poverty. *American Behavioral Scientist, 34*(4), 416–430.

Garmezy, N. (1992, August). *Vulnerability and resilience.* Presentation at the 100th annual meeting of the American Psychological Association, Washington, DC.

Gerber, P. J., Ginsberg, R. J., & Reiff, H. B. (1990). *Identifying alterable patterns in employment success for highly successful adults with learning disabilities* (Final Report H133G80500). Washington, DC: National Institute on Disability Research and Rehabilitation, Department of Education.

Goleman, D. (1995). *Emotional intelligence.* New York: Bantam.

Hechtman, L. (1991). Resilience and vulnerability in long-term outcome of attention-deficit/hyperactivity disorder. *Canadian Journal of Psychiatry, 36,* 415–421.

James, B. (1989). *Treating traumatized children: New insights and creative interventions.* New York: Lexington.

Janoff-Bulman, R. (1992). *Shattered assumptions: Towards a new psychology of trauma.* New York: Free.

Jones, C. (1994). *Attention deficit disorder: Strategies for school-age children.* Tucson: Communication Skill Builders.

Katz, M. (1994, May). From challenged childhood to achieving adulthood: Studies in resilience. *CH.A.D.D. Newsletter,* 8–11.

Katz-Leavy, J., Lourie, I., Stroul, B., & Zeigler-Dendy, C. (1992). *Individualized services in a system of care.* Washington, DC: CASSP Technical Assistance Center, Center For Child Health and Mental Health Policy, Georgetown University Child Development Center.

Kennedy, D. (1992, December 13). Crack babies' lives need not be wasted; here's living proof. *San Diego Union,* pp. 31–33.

Kinsbourne, M. (1993, October). *The quality of life for those with ADD.* Presentation at the fifth annual conference of CH.A.D.D. (Children and Adults with Attention Deficit Disorder), San Diego.

Kirk, J. (1992, September/October). Ivory tower meets the elementary school classroom: University and district combine efforts to serve children with ADD. *The Special Edge,* 8–11.

Kiser, L. J., Heston, J., Millsap, P. A., & Pruitt, D. B. (1991). Physical and sexual abuse in childhood: Relationship with post-traumatic stress disorder. *Journal of the American Academy of Child and Adolescent Psychiatry, 30*(5), 776–783.

Kline, A. (1993, February). *A voice of experience.* Presentation at the international conference of Learning Disabilities Association of America, San Francisco.

Kotkin, R. (1994, October). *Serving children with ADD in the regular classsroom: The Irvine Paraprofessional Model.* Table Top Discussions at the sixth annual conference of CH.A.D.D. (Children and Adults with Attention Deficit Disorder), New York.

Kotulak, R. (1993, December 12). Tracking down the monster within: Genes of aggression found. *Chicago Tribune,* pp. 22–23.

Lavoie, R. (1989). *Understanding learning disabilities: How difficult can this be?* [video]. Alexandria, VA: P.B.S. Video.

Lavoie, R. (1992a, March). *Tales from the front.* Presentation at the international conference of Learning Disabilities Association of America, Atlanta.

Lavoie, R. (1992b). *Integrating learning disabled students: Linguisystems Audio Workshops.* East Moline, IL: LinguiSystems.

Lewis, B. (1992). *Kids with courage: True stories about young people making a difference.* Minneapolis: Free Spirit.

Lowe, P. (1993). *Carepooling: How to get the help you need to care for the ones you love.* San Francisco: Berett-Koehler.

Lyons, J. A. (1987). Post-traumatic stress disorder in children: A review of the literature. *Developmental and Behavioral Pediatrics, 8*(6), 349–356.

McCormick, P. (1993, October). How kids survive trauma. *Parents,* 71–74.

McLaughlin, M. W., Irby, M. A., & Langman, J. (1994). *Urban sanctuaries: Neighborhood organizations in the lives and futures of inner-city youth.* San Francisco: Jossey-Bass.

McLeer, S. V., Deblinger, E., Henry, D., & Orvaschel, H. (1992). Sexually abused children at high risk for posttraumatic stress disorder. *Journal of the Academy of Child and Adolescent Psychiatry, 3*(5), 875–879.

McNight, J. (1989). Do no harm: Policy options that meet human needs. *Social Policy, 5,* 5–15.

Mills, J. (1993). A little piece of mind. On *Urgent Reply: Creating New Understandings of the ADD/At Risk Experience* [CD]. Marquette, MI: Impulse Presentatations.

National Commission On Children. (1991). *Beyond rhetoric: A new American agenda for children and families* (Final report, pp. 213–214). Washington, DC: Author.

Neskahi, A. (1995, April). *Fostering resiliency in kids and working with American Indian youth in the school setting.* Presentation at the Conference on Resiliency in Children and Families, Helena, Montana: Intermountain Children's Home, Casey Family Program, and the Summit Project.

Pennebaker, J. W., & Beall, S. K. (1986). Confronting a traumatic event: Toward an understanding of inhibition and disease. *Journal of Abnormal Psychology, 95*(3), 274–281.

Peschel, E., Peschel, R., Howe, C. W., & Howe, J. W. (Eds.). (1992, Summer). *Neurobiological disorders in children and adolescents* (pp. 1–5). San Francisco: Jossey-Bass.

Peterson, C., Maier, S. F., & Seligman, M. E. P. (1993). *Learned helplessness: A theory for the age of personal control.* New York: Oxford University.

Phillips, B. W. (1993). Intervention opportunities: Ignore child abuse now, attend to adult social problems later. *The Brown University Child and Adolescent Behavior Letter, 9*(10), 1–4.

Pynoos, R. (1991). *Understanding psychological trauma: Part III. Healing our children* [5-part video series]. Urbana, IL: Baxley Media Group.

Rachman, S. (1979). The concept of required helpfulness. *Behavior Research and Therapy, 17,* 1–6.

Rakos R., & Schroeder, H. (1976). Fear reduction in help-givers as a function of helping. *Journal of Counseling Psychology, 23,* 428–435.

Raphael, B. (1991). *Understanding psychological trauma: Part III. Healing our children* [5-part video series]. Urbana, IL: Baxley Media Group.

Rutter, M. (1979a). *Fifteen thousand hours: Secondary schools and their effects on children.* Cambridge: Harvard University Press.

Rutter, M. (1979b). Protective factors in children's responses to stress and disadvantage. In M. W. Kent & J. E. Rolf (Eds.), *Primary Prevention of Psychopathology* (Vol. 3, pp. 49–74). Hanover, NH, University Press of New England.

Rutter, M. (1990). Psychosocial resilience and protective mechanisms. In J. Rolf, A. S. Masten, D. Cicchetti, K. H. Nuechterlein, & S. Weintraub (Eds.), *Risk and protective factors in the development of psychopathology* (pp. 181–214). New York: Cambridge University.

Rutter, M., Quinton, D., & Hill, J. (1990). Adult outcome of institution-reared children: Males and females compared. In L. Robins & M. Rutter (Eds.), *Straight and deviant pathways from childhood to adulthood* (pp. 135–157). Cambridge: Cambridge University.

Rutter, M., & Rutter, M. (1993). *Developing minds: Challenge and continuity across the lifespan.* New York: Basic.

Sameroff, A. (1992). *Abuse and neglect of children: Risk and resilience.* Time to Grow: A Television Based Course in Child Development:

Infancy through Adolescence. Fountain Valley, CA: Coast Community College District.

Schorr, L. (1988). *Within our reach: Breaking the cycle of disadvantage.* New York: Anchor.

Seligman, M. E. P. (1995). *The optimistic child.* New York: Houghton Mifflin.

Shure, M. (1992). *I can problem solve: An interpersonal cognitive problem solving program.* Champaign, IL: Research.

Silvern, D. (1994, March 24). "Bald eagles" thrilled by hair-raising news of classmate. *San Diego Union Tribune,* pp. B1, B3.

Smith, S. (1994). *Different is not bad, different is the world.* Longmont, CO: Sopris West.

Smith, S. (1993). *Color me successful: The Lab School of Washington Outstanding Learning Dsiabled Achiever Awards 1985-1993.* Washington, DC: The Lab School.

Spekman, N. J., Goldberg, R. J., & Herman, K. L. (1992). Learning disabled children grow up: A search for factors related to success in the young adult years. *Learning Disabilities Research and Practice, 7,* 161–170.

Stampp, K. M. (1956). *The peculiar institution.* New York: Knopf.

Strain, P., Steele, P., Ellis, T., & Timm, M. (1982). Long-term effects of oppositional child treatment with mothers as therapists and therapist trainers. *Journal of Applied Behavior Analysis, 7,* 583–590.

Strain, P., Young, C., & Horowitz, J. (1981). An examination of child and family demographic variables related to generalized behavior change during oppositional child training. *Behavior Modification, 5,* 15–26.

Tannen, N. (1993, April). *Families first.* Presentation at the second annual Wraparound Conference, St. Charles, IL.

Taylor, S. E. (1989). *Positive illusions: Creative self deception and the healthy mind.* New York: Basic.

Terr, L. (1990). *Too scared to cry.* New York: Basic.

Thompson, S. C. (1985). Finding positive meaning in a stressful event. *Basic and Applied Social Psychology, 6,* 279–295.

Timm, M. (1993). The regional intervention program: Family treatment by family members. *Journal of the Council for Children with Behavioral Disorders, 19*(1), 34–43.

van der Kolk, B. A. (1994). *Trauma and development in children* [video]. New York: Bureau of Psychiatric Services, New York State Department of Mental Health.

van der Kolk, B. A., & Greenberg, M. S. (1987). The psychobiology of the trauma response: Hyperarousal, constriction and addiction to traumatic reexposure. In van der Kolk, B. A. (Ed.), *Psychological Trauma* (pp. 63–89). Washington, DC: American Psychiatric Press.

VanDenBerg, J. E. (1992, Summer). Individualized services for children. In E. Peschel, R. Peschel, R. C. W. Howe, & J. W. Howe (Eds.),

Neurobiological disorders in children and adolescents (pp. 97–100). San Francisco: Jossey-Bass.

Weiner, B. (1993). On sin versus sickness: A theory of perceived responsibility and social motivation. *AmericanPsychologist, 48*(9), 957–965.

Weiss, G., & Trokenberg-Hechtman, L. (1993). *Hyperactive children grown up: ADHD in children, adolescents and adults.* New York: Guilford.

Welch, M. B. (1993). *The touch of the master's hand.* In J. Canfield, & M. V. Hansen, *Chicken Soup for the Soul.* Deerfield Beach, FL: Heath Communications.

Wender, P. H. (1987). *The hyperactive child, adolescent and adult: Attention deficit disorder through the lifespan.* New York: Oxford.

Werner, E. (1993, February). *A longitudinal perspective on risk for learning disabilities.* Presentation at the international conference of the Learning Disability Association of America, San Francisco.

Werner, E. (1995). Resilience in development. *Current Directions in Psychological Science, American Psychological Society, 4*(5), 81–85.

Werner, E., & Smith, R. (1992). *Overcoming the odds: High-risk children from birth to adulthoood.* Ithaca, NY: Cornell University.

White, M., & Epston, D. (1990). *Narrative means to therapeutic ends.* New York: Norton.

Wolfe, V. V., Gentile, C., & Wolfe, D. A. (1989). The impact of sexual abuse on children: A PTSD formulation. *Behavior Therapy, 20,* 215–228.

Wolin, S. J., & Wolin, S. W. (1993). *The resilient self: How survivors of troubled families rise above adversity.* New York: Villard.

Wolin, S. J., & Wolin, S. W. (1994). *Survivor's pride: Building resilience in youth at risk* [video]. Verona, WI: The Attainment Company.

Zimrin, H. (1986). A profile of survival. *Child Abuse and Neglect, 10,* 339–349.

Index